MISS *the* MARK:

Don't Take the Mark of the Beast!

By Apostle Stan Johnson

ISBN# 978-0-578-62074-9

Printed and bound
in the United States of America

First Printing, January 2020

Printed by:
Kingery Printing Company
3012 S. Banker Street
Effingham, IL 62401

www.prophecyclub.com

All scriptures are from the
Authorized King James Bible.

*This book has been purposely made thin
using near-Bible paper, in the typical Bible size of 6 x 9
to make it easy to carry with your Bible as a handy reference.

_____   _____
                 Name   Date

_____
         #

Table of Contents

PREFACE

This Supernatural Book

This is a supernatural book. I didn't just decide to write this book. It was on my heart, but God spoke to a Prophet and showed her the NAME of the book, the TITLE of the book and what the COVER of the BOOK should look like. That Prophet just happened to be my wife, Leslie.

God began to speak to my heart to research the Mark of the Beast with urgency, as this event will come soon. The research I conducted led me to do two broadcasts. A few days later, God gave my wife, Leslie, the dream confirming this book. This was a great confirmation to me. This was what she saw in her dream:

MISS THE MARK:
Dream given to Prophet Leslie Johnson, Stan's wife–
Saturday, June 22, 2019

"I dreamed I was talking with Stan. I was telling him the overall bottom line message of end time prophecy is to let the world know not to take the "Mark of the Beast." I was telling him the feasts and all the good information he has in his first book ***"Secret Door to Understand Bible Prophecy"*** is good, but very deep. For many people it takes a while to sink in, for a person new to Bible prophecy. It is like, "pass the potatoes" to Stan. I told him he is the "walking/talking Bible prophecy man," and understanding Bible prophecies is simpler for him than others. It is a hunger and thirst he walks in daily. God gives him supernatural revelation whereas for most new people it takes study to understand.

"Then, I saw the cover of his new book. I saw the name, it was, "Miss the Mark." I saw the spiral-like target which Stan is always seeing everywhere he goes, which is a hidden 666. The body of the spiral-666 was a snake looking serpent. I saw an arrow fly by missing the 666-spiral-target to "Missing the Mark.""

The tip of the arrow hit the Bible in the center. The tip of the arrow was an open Bible. The Bible was opened with a bright light shining out of it."

~Prophet Leslie Johnson

I took this as confirmation I was to write this book. The title is to be, "Miss the Mark." I want this book to be a simple way to understand the end times with the goal to get this book into many hands that would convince them not to take the "Mark of the Beast." They will not take it if they understand the consequences.

ABOUT THE BOOK COVER

On the left side of the cover of the book it had, at first glance, what appeared to be an archery target. This is NOT an archery target. Below is a picture of an archery target. It has 10 rings and a center or "bullseye." The outside two rings were white, the next two were black, the next two were blue, the next two were red, and the inside 3 were yellow with a "+" mark.

The image on the front of this book is NOT an official target. It is a hidden "Number of the Beast" or "666." Red and white appear to be a target but it's not really a target.

Remember, Satan was the most subtle beast of the field. Our conscious mind can reject ideas but our subconscious can't. Things we see but our conscious mind does not eliminate go into our subconscious mind. Experts tell us our conscious mind forgets easily but our subconscious mind never forgets.

I believe the reason these are sprinkled subtlety with the spiral in the background of television, movies, restaurants, pictures, drawings, signs is to pre-program the subconscious mind to accept it. Unknowingly we have already accepted the "number of his name." The image on the front of this book is the "number of his name."

TRUST JESUS WITH OUR DEATH

Those who have accepted Jesus as their Lord have decided to trust Jesus with their eternity. They believe that He died and rose again so He can resurrect them as well. They trust Him with their eternity.

Those who have accepted Jesus as their Lord also trust Jesus to care for them daily. They trust Him with their daily provisions, their jobs, and families. They trust Him with their daily lives.

I want to challenge all believers to also trust Jesus with their death. Jesus has the keys of hell and death. He decides the very moment our heart stops beating and how. He decides who goes to heaven and who goes to hell. I say we must trust Jesus with our death! We must believe that Jesus will see to it that not more than what we can take is placed upon us. He is not going to put so much upon us that we will not succeed. Success can be found in our death as well as in our life and eternity!

1CO 10:13 There hath no temptation taken you but such as is common to man: but God is faithful, who will NOT SUFFER YOU TO BE TEMPTED ABOVE THAT YE ARE ABLE; but will with the temptation also make a way to escape, that YE MAY BE ABLE TO BEAR IT.

If we can trust Jesus in our death, life, and eternity, then it matters not when the rapture is, nor when or how death comes! Those who have not read my book, **"The Secret Door to Understand Bible Prophecy,"** do not yet understand the chronological order of the last days events. They probably love Jesus very much but lack information. They believe Jesus is going to come before any trouble and pull them in the air to keep them from experiencing any trouble or tribulation. Others think the event happens more in the middle of the Tribulation. Others believe it happens just before the end. The timing of the end, is one of the 30 revelations I received which is in my book, **"The Secret Door to Understand Bible Prophecy."** I was shown The Rapture happens on the Day of the Lord which occurs on the last Feast, the Day of Trumpets, which will be the last day of sin , and the last day of the Tribulation. Look at the charts at the back of this book to understand them, get **"The Secret Door to Understand Bible Prophecy."**

If the rapture were to take place before the Tribulation, who would be forced to take the Mark of the Beast? This verse says the Beast FORCES people to take the Mark. If all the Christians are taken out who will he FORCE to take the Mark? No one! All those remaining would be sinners or foolish virgins. They will easily take the Mark! They will not know the warning– the danger– the consequences. To those who have not accepted Christ it will sound like a reasonable thing to do! Only those who have read Revelation 13 will resist!!! Only the Christians! This will be our final test!

REV 13:16 And HE CAUSETH all, both small and great, rich and poor, free and bond, to receive a mark in their right hand, or in their foreheads:

INTRODUCTION:

QUICK OVERVIEW

Before the heavens and the earth were created, God the Father knowing all, gave Jesus His Son the Book of Life. In it were written the names of every person on earth who were given to Jesus to be his people to live eternally with him.

Mankind was assigned about 6 thousand years to give each person time to determine their place in eternity. For the purpose of this book, we are discussing the last seven years before it all concludes with the final return of Jesus to destroy the old earth, and the evil people in it, and make a new heaven and a new earth in which those whose name is in the Book of Life will live eternally.

The last seven years before the end is called the "Tribulation." It comes on the earth like a woman having a baby. At first, the birth pains are small and far apart gradually increasing in pain and intensity until the new creation arrives.

Likewise, the old earth is now in those early birth pains. I believe they started on December 26, 2004 with the great tsunami which killed over 160,000 people in Banda Ache, Thailand.

Right after the Tsunami hit, I gave a sermon. In an instant, faster than the blink of an eye I was made to know, "This is the breaking of the water." The earth is now in travail as a woman with child concluding with the return of Jesus. Even today, I could take you to the very spot in the carpet and show you exactly where I was standing when this happened.

This was the "breaking of the water" signaling the birth pains upon the world have begun. These birth pains will continue to get worse according to the Book of Revelation. By the time the end arrives, it will be the worst time on earth.

At the conclusion of the Tribulation, a new eternal Kingdom will be set up for those who obtain it in which there will be happiness and eternal life. In that you are reading this book is a high probability your name is in the Book of Life. But now you need to make sure. You need to ask Jesus to forgive your sins.

One of the first signals the last seven years has arrived is when the people of the world form a world government. The leaders of the earth will divide the seven continents into ten global regions. One of the regional leaders will overcome three of the other leaders. This will be "The Beast." He will be the most handsome intelligent man to ever live on the earth but also the evilest. Even worse, God gives him a special speaking ability. He will be the best speaker on earth and will say very bad lies about God, the Bible, the people in the Bible, and all religions on earth.

He will destroy the religious beliefs of almost all people on earth no matter what race or religion. He will speak with such eloquence that unless your name is already in the Book of Life, most people will accept this man as the Truth, the New Messiah, the true man-god, and be eventually tossed into the Lake of Fire being tormented forever.

After he destroys the beliefs of every other religion on earth, almost all people will worship him as god. This will be the worst thing you can do in your life! If you accept this man you will be tormented in great pain and suffering for all eternity. Don't make the greatest of all mistakes by worshiping him, his image, receiving his Mark, or the number of his name. It won't be easy to resist; hence "overcomer."

The purpose of this book is to help you recognize the Beast, his image, his mark, and the number of his name and to refuse it.

Chapter 1

What is the Mark of the Beast?

We don't exactly know what the mark looks like. We have two hints. We know it is a Mark put in either the right hand or on the forehead but there are four things we want to make certain NOT to accept, in Rev. 14:9-11.

THE WORST THING THAT CAN HAPPEN

According to the Book of Revelation, the worst thing that can happen to you in your entire life is to accept one of the following: The Beast; his image; his Mark; or the number of his name.

REV 15:2, And I saw as it were a sea of glass mingled with fire: and them that had gotten the victory over THE BEAST, and over HIS IMAGE, and over HIS MARK, and over THE NUMBER OF HIS NAME, stand on the sea of glass, having the harps of God.

Those whose name is not in the Book of Life are cast into the Lake of Fire. They will get soul-death, destroying both soul and body. Their torment, their constant pain, will end. They will be as they had not been [Obadiah 1:16]. But those taking the Mark, worshiping his image, receiving his Mark, or the number of his name NEVER DIE. They do not get soul-death. They are tormented day and night forever in the Lake of Fire and brimstone. They have no hope of escape, no water, no food, terrible smells, torture by the devil's demons,

and they will be there by their own mistake. They were deceived, but it was their decision to make. They decided to believe the Beast!

REV 20:10, And the devil that deceived them was cast into the lake of fire and brimstone, where the beast and the false prophet are, and shall be TORMENTED DAY AND NIGHT FOR EVER AND EVER.

REV 14:9-11, ...If any man worship the beast and his image, and receive his mark in his forehead, or in his hand, The same shall drink of the wine of the wrath of God, which is poured out without mixture into the cup of his indignation; and he shall be tormented with fire and brimstone in the presence of the holy angels, and in the presence of the Lamb: And THE SMOKE OF THEIR TORMENT ASCENDETH UP FOR EVER AND EVER: AND THEY HAVE NO REST DAY NOR NIGHT, who worship the beast and his image, and whosoever receiveth the mark of his name.

Mark Twain said, "It is easier to deceive someone than to convince them they are deceived."

I heard it said, "There is only one true barrier to the truth, the conviction you already have it."

The strange thing about deception is the person deceived, DOESN'T KNOW IT!

It is my opinion the only accurate English version of the Bible is the King James Bible. All others have errors. If we accept even one error, many others will follow. We must run after Truth with all our strength. We must refuse to compromise.

REV 14:9-11, ...If any man worship the beast and his image, and receive his mark in his forehead, or in his hand, The same shall drink of the wine of the wrath of God, which is poured out without mixture into the cup of his indignation; and he shall be tormented with fire and brimstone in the presence of the holy angels, and in the presence of the Lamb: And THE SMOKE OF THEIR TORMENT ASCENDETH UP FOR EVER AND EVER: AND THEY HAVE NO REST DAY NOR NIGHT, who worship the beast and his image, and whosoever receiveth the mark of his name.

THE IMAGE OF THE BEAST:

Many scriptures speak of a time when the people of the world create images or idols to worship. They will make small replicas of the Beast and/or his image to worship. Many idols will be made.

Scriptures say the False Prophet will command an image of the Beast to be made. Then he will command all the world to worship it or be killed. Many will die for Jesus.

They will say this is the new true religion, the true messiah. All who refuse will be the "unbelievers" (those who truly serve Jesus will refuse his image). The image will command all the "true believers" to kill all "unbelievers" and all whose names that are not ALREADY written in the Book of Life WILL convert or be killed.

Imagine all those whose names are not in the Book of Life, those not already Christians, turning at once against all the Christians. Imagine the Beast, the ultimate authority and lawgiver, issuing orders to all the so called "true believers" (not Christians) to kill all the unbelievers (the true believers)! They hunt down and kill all the unbelievers– all those without the Mark of the Beast!

This is the primary reason you must quickly ask Jesus into your heart now, before you see or hear the Beast. Once you see or hear him, you will be hooked (drawn to his beauty), and it will be very difficult to resist. The Bible says the deception will be so good that, "if it were possible even the elect would be deceived."

DAN 7:21, I beheld, and the same horn [the Beast] MADE WAR WITH THE SAINTS, and prevailed against them;

DAN 7:8, ...a mouth speaking great things.

REV 13:5, And there was given unto him A MOUTH SPEAKING GREAT THINGS and blasphemies; and power was given unto him to continue forty and two months. [3½ years] And he opened his mouth in blasphemy [Direct attack against God] against God, to blaspheme his name, and his tabernacle, and them that dwell in heaven. And it was given unto him TO MAKE WAR WITH THE SAINTS, AND TO OVERCOME THEM: and power was given him over all kindreds, and tongues, and nations. And ALL THAT DWELL UPON THE EARTH SHALL WORSHIP HIM, whose names are not written in the BOOK OF LIFE of the Lamb slain from the foundation of the world.

REV 13:15, And HE HAD POWER TO GIVE LIFE UNTO THE IMAGE OF THE BEAST, that the image of the beast should both SPEAK, and CAUSE that as many as would not worship the image of the beast should be KILLED.

THE MARK:

The Bible says the mark involves the number 666 or six-hundred, three-score and six.

REVELATION 13:16, "And he causeth all, both small and great, rich and poor, free and bond, to receive a MARK in their RIGHT HAND, or in their FOREHEADS: And that NO MAN MIGHT BUY OR SELL, save he that had the MARK, or the NAME of the beast, or the NUMBER OF HIS NAME. Here is wisdom. Let him that hath understanding count the number of the beast: for it is the number of a man; and his number is Six hundred threescore and six. [666]"

In May of 2000, The Prophecy Club had Ken Peters speak about a dream he had twenty-five years earlier about the night God called him to be a Prophet. The title of the DVD is ***"I Saw the Tribulation"*** [DVD available at **ProphecyClub.com**; watch instantly at **WatchProphecyClub.com**]. He tells of how he lived through the first three and one-half years of the Tribulation until he was beheaded for Christ. Out of 330 DVDs made over 25 years, it is still to this day one of our most popular. He said some amazing things, and no one I know doubts it is true. Ken Peters said, "The Antichrist was the most handsome man I have ever seen." The Scriptures tell us he looks different than normal humans. Perhaps it is because he is genetically different from us.

The Bible says a thing is established when two or three people testify to the same thing. Ken is the only person who has seen this image, so it is NOT confirmed. This may NOT be the Mark of the Beast. For now, it is

Ken Peters said, "The Mark of the Beast was about the size of a U.S. nickel. It was located in the web between the thumb and first finger and looked like the yellow Mexico sun with another hand in the middle of the sun." He saw no chip associated with it, just a tattoo.

the best information we have. Soon, all the world will have the opportunity to find out.

> DEUTERONOMY 19:15, *"...at the mouth of TWO WITNESSES, or at the mouth of THREE WITNESSES, shall the matter be ESTABLISHED."*

He further went to state that, "The Mark of the Beast was about the size of a U.S. nickel. It was located in the web between the thumb and first finger and looked like the yellow Mexico sun with another hand in the middle of the sun." Ken said he did not see any computer chip attached with it at all. Either that goes on the right hand, or on the forehead one, or the other and that fits perfectly with scripture. I do not think that there's going to be a computer chip inserted under our skin. I think WE ALREADY HAVE THE COMPUTER CHIP! Please allow me to explain.

TRIBULATION DREAM: Prophet Maurice Sklar Saturday, March 15, 2014,

"I saw multitudes of Tribulation saints refusing to renounce Jesus as LORD. They were starving, many of them, but still refused to take the stamp on their bodies so they could eat and live. There was what looked like kiosks that were in every little town. They advertised food and water, only if you went inside them and took the electronic mark. Some went in, bowed down to a holographic movie image of the Antichrist and were branded in their hands and foreheads with an electronic tattoo-like stamp.

When they came out, if they came out, they had a zombie-like look.

Their minds and souls were gone. It looked like they had a spiritual lobotomy. Then these immediately joined the armies of those police units, and were given weapons after they were fed, and drank, and rested in the kiosk. They were like robots doing the Antichrist's bidding. I knew that they were lost forever. But, quite a few did not make it out. They were tortured mentally and physically inside the kiosk thing, but, if they still refused the Mark of the beast, there was a laser that shot through their brain and heart, and sliced their heads off. Then they were immediately incinerated. Nothing but ashes remained. This was the most horrifying of all. It made the Nazi death camps look like a picnic, if that is possible. Millions of people were executed in this way via computer systems automatically with such precision and efficiency that I marveled that something like this was even possible and could take place on such a large scale. The technology was more advanced than I had ever seen."

~Maurice Sklar

THE NUMBER OF HIS NAME: SPIRAL

Satan is the subtlest beast of the field. I see this spiral placed subtly almost everywhere. In my opinion, it is probably the number of his name.

Let's ask ourselves, "How can we make the numbers 666 very subtle? Still there, but very subtle?"

Like this: not only is the 666 hidden in these spirals, but it is also the story of "progressive evil." At first a person does evil. They are still a long

way from Lucifer. That represents the outer edges of the spiral. As a person gets progressively evil, they get closer to the devil.

This spiral is found on food, movies, logos, television, hotels, restaurants, clothes, magazines, books, and even children's cartoons! For this reason, I believe this has the highest probability of being the "number of his name."

THERE ARE FOUR THINGS THAT WE MUST AVOID.

I am going to ask you a question and most of you reading this will probably get it wrong. Do you think that you'll take the Mark of the Beast?

I am sure you are now saying, "No! Absolutely not!"

Are you sure?

If you have not done your research, if you don't understand the deceptions of the Beast, you could very well take the Mark of the Beast!

We must remember, the devil has been around for over 6,000 years and he is far smarter than any human on earth. He has tricked the best humans,

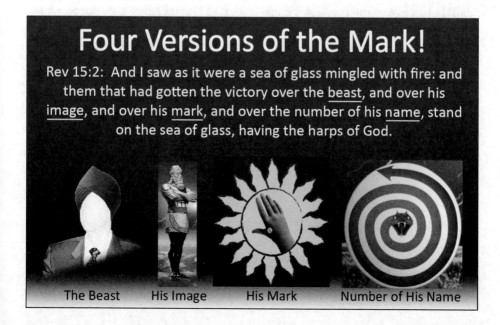

Four Versions of the Mark!

Rev 15:2: And I saw as it were a sea of glass mingled with fire: and them that had gotten the victory over the beast, and over his image, and over his mark, and over the number of his name, stand on the sea of glass, having the harps of God.

The Beast   His Image   His Mark   Number of His Name

right? He has a plan he has been putting in place and setting up for 6,000 years! He has nine deceptions we know of. They will be so powerful and so complete that only a few, only those whose names are in the Book of Life will refuse all of them! It only takes one deception for you to fall! Just one! And many are coming!

He has a well thought out, well-planned deception to trick almost everyone on the earth into taking the Mark of the Beast, worshiping his image, or receiving the number of his name or thereof. That's the best way to say it to keep it simple.

MAT 24:24, For there shall arise false Christs, and false prophets, and shall shew great signs and wonders; insomuch that, if it were possible, they shall deceive the very elect.

So, we must open our eyes, ears and we must be informed, or we could fall.

I believe we are the last generation. And as the last generation, most of us will have the opportunity to deny Jesus in our lifetime. So, the best time to decide that we're not going to fall, we're not going to deny Jesus is not when we are in the shadow of the Guillotine. It is not when we are on our knees with our hands tied behind our back and the enemy is saying, "Deny him or you will die!" It is now, as you read this book! You should have already made your decision before that moment!

Thinking the decision through now. Deciding NOW we will make the correct decision before then! We have already decided, we are not going to take it. This book, led by the Holy Spirit, is going to help us make that decision now.

We are about to cover the most terrifying events humankind will face. If we want to sleep at night and have a relatively normal life, we must decide we will trust Jesus with our death!

Jesus will not forgive us for taking the Mark!

In a later chapter, I will explain the greatest deceptions in human history. This includes the space show, the archaeology deception, the rapture deception, create life, deception by miracles, the alien revelation, super-humans, no man might buy or sell, and the economic crash. Those are all plans of Satan.

Chapter 2

The Beast

APPEARANCE: HANDSOME

More about the Beast. The Beast will be the most handsome, most beautiful, most intelligent, man in human history! The Book of Daniel says, "his look is more STOUT than his fellows." Stout means great or abundant. Daniel also says he has a "fierce countenance" meaning a strong, fierce, mighty or a powerful look.

Ken Peters said he was the most beautiful man he had ever seen. Maurice Sklar saw him and said, "He was the most handsome or beautiful man I have ever seen."

The objective of the Beast will be to deceive all religions, especially Christians, and replace them with his one-world religion that will worship him. Some people call it the New World Order.

DAN 7:20, And of the ten horns that were in his head, and of the other which came up, and before whom three fell; even of that horn that had eyes, and a mouth that spake very great things, whose LOOK WAS MORE STOUT THAN HIS FELLOWS.

DAN 8:23, And in the latter time of their kingdom, when the transgressors are come to the full, a king of FIERCE COUNTENANCE, and understanding dark sentences, shall stand up.

MOUTH FROM GOD:

He will be the most eloquent speaking man in human history. The Book of Revelation says God gives him a supernatural mouth speaking the greatest [not good] things against Christ, His Church, and His tabernacle. He will completely destroy all religions except the overcomer Christians. He will be able to answer any question including those of the origins of the universe, earth, and religion. The Beast will give such amazing answers that the world will WONDER at his words! They will say no one on earth has ever spoken like this! A man with all the answers! Finally, we understand why there are so many divisions between nations, so many wars, so many religions! To have true peace on earth, they will command all people to unite against those refusing to join the new society and kill them. All who resist the Mark shall be killed.

To the Muslims, he will be the Mahdi. To the Hindus, he will be the Vishnu. To the Christian, he will be the Christ. Lastly, to the Jews, the Messiah! Pretty much only those whose name is in the Book of Life BEFORE they see and hear the Beast, will escape and overcome him.

On the outside, he will appear to have all the answers, but his heart is full of the devil– literally! He initially obtains his kingdom by compliment or flatteries. Then he will defeat three other regional world leaders. He will say all the world can be at peace if you just abandon all the old myths, laws, and religions by joining his new world [with him as world ruler].

> *DAN 11:21, And in his estate shall stand up a vile person, to whom they shall not give the honour of the kingdom: but HE SHALL COME IN PEACEABLY, and obtain the kingdom by flatteries.*

> *DAN 7:8, I considered the horns, and, behold, there came up among them another LITTLE HORN, [the Beast] before whom there were three of the first horns plucked up by the roots...*

Israel will accept the Beast as Messiah! Really!

> *JOH 5:43, I am come in my Father's name, and ye receive me not: if ANOTHER SHALL COME IN HIS OWN NAME, HIM YE WILL RECEIVE.*

He will claim he is the one and only true God.

> *DAN 11:36-37, And the king shall do according to his will; and HE SHALL EXALT HIMSELF, AND MAGNIFY HIMSELF ABOVE EVERY GOD, and shall SPEAK MARVELLOUS [BAD] THINGS AGAINST THE GOD OF GODS, and shall prosper till the indignation be accomplished: for that that is determined shall be done. Neither shall he regard the God of his fathers, nor the desire of women, nor regard any god: for HE SHALL MAGNIFY HIMSELF ABOVE ALL.*

Because most of the world has rejected free salvation through the finished sacrifice of Jesus. God will send them a strong delusion/deception which they will believe and be destroyed.

> *2TH 2:3-12, Let no man deceive you by any means: for that day* [Return of Christ] *shall not come, except there come a falling away first,* [Defection from the truth] *and that man of sin* [The Antichrist/Beast] *be revealed, the son of perdition;* [Perdition is eternal life in torment.] *Who opposeth and exalteth himself above all that is called God, or that is worshipped; so that he as God sitteth in the temple of God, SHEWING HIMSELF THAT HE IS GOD.* [The Antichrist appears to be Christ but has deceived people into thinking so.] ... *And then shall that Wicked* [Beast] *be revealed, whom the Lord shall consume with the spirit of his mouth, and shall destroy with the brightness of his coming:* [Morning Star-Light-sword] *Even him, whose coming is after the working of Satan* [Satan gives him his power] *with ALL POWER AND SIGNS AND LYING WONDERS,* [Deceptions from heaven] *And with all deceivableness of unrighteousness in them that perish; BECAUSE THEY RECEIVED NOT THE LOVE OF THE TRUTH, THAT THEY MIGHT BE SAVED. AND FOR THIS CAUSE GOD SHALL SEND THEM STRONG DELUSION, THAT THEY SHOULD BELIEVE A LIE: THAT THEY ALL MIGHT BE DAMNED WHO BELIEVED NOT THE TRUTH, BUT HAD PLEASURE IN UNRIGHTEOUSNESS.*

Expect the Beast to use scripture, prophecies, and ancient text to crush the foundations of all beliefs, especially Christianity! Expect the Beast to duplicate Christ, Mohammed, Buddha, Krishna, and merge all religious leaders into himself as the fulfillment of all of them! Expect him to explain, not only the Bible and ancient mysteries, but give an answer to almost all of mankind's questions.

DAN 8:23-25, And in the latter time of their kingdom, when the transgressors are come to the full, a king of fierce countenance, and UNDERSTAND-ING DARK SENTENCES, shall stand up. And his power shall be mighty, but not by his own power: [Dragon gives him power] *and he shall destroy wonderfully, and shall prosper, and practise, and shall destroy the mighty and the holy people. And through his policy also he shall cause craft* [Evil] *to prosper in his hand; and he shall magnify himself in his heart,* ["I am God"] *and by peace* [He will say by forming a world government and all worshiping him the world can finally be at peace.] *shall destroy many: he shall also stand up against the Prince of princes;* [Jesus] *but he shall be broken without hand.* [Jesus uses the light-sword out of his mouth to destroy all the wicked.]

Chapter 3

If I Take The Mark, Will I Lose My Salvation?

There was a time when I believed in "once saved– always saved." Meaning, if you accept Christ you can never ever go to hell. I found the following verses which say a person CAN lose their salvation by turning from righteousness.

EZE 3:18-20, When I say unto the wicked, Thou shalt surely die; and thou givest him not warning, nor speakest to warn the wicked from his wicked way, to save his life; the same wicked man shall die in his iniquity ...if thou warn the wicked, and he turn not from his wickedness, nor from his wicked way, he shall die in his iniquity ...WHEN A RIGHTEOUS MAN DOTH TURN FROM HIS RIGHTEOUSNESS, AND COMMIT INIQUITY, AND I LAY A STUMBLINGBLOCK BEFORE HIM, HE SHALL DIE: because thou hast not given him warning, HE SHALL DIE IN HIS SIN, AND HIS RIGHTEOUSNESS WHICH HE HATH DONE SHALL NOT BE REMEMBERED; but his blood will I require at thine hand.

EXO 32:33, And the LORD said unto Moses, Whosoever hath sinned against me, HIM WILL I BLOT OUT OF MY BOOK.

In Revelation, the definition of overcomer is one who sees and hears the Beast but does not accept him.

The New Testament says overcomers won't get their name blotted out, indirectly saying that a person CAN be removed from the Book of Life therefore losing their salvation, especially for taking the Mark of the Beast.

REV 3:5, He that overcometh, the same shall be clothed in white raiment; and I WILL NOT BLOT OUT HIS NAME OUT OF THE BOOK OF LIFE, but I will confess his name before my Father, and before his angels.

DO NOT TAKE THE MARK, DAUGHTER!

When God first called me to start the Prophecy Club radio program in 1993, my wife asked to speak with me. I can still remember the very seats we sat in at the kitchen table. She said, "If anyone ever threatens you with me or the children do NOT give in. We do NOT belong to you. We belong to God. You only have temporary oversight over us. Do NOT give in for us." I hadn't considered that, but it brought comfort! I suggest you have a similar conversation with your loves ones.

Dale Carnegie says, "Ask yourself: What is the worst that can happen? Accept it and try to improve on it."

Envision the worst thing, would be in a line with our children, heading to the guillotine, then the man with a clipboard steps up and says, "Mr. Johnson, this is your last opportunity to step out of line. If you deny Him, [they never say his name] you will receive good treatment, food, shower, clean clothes, and a bed. If you do not, you will continue to stand in line [Heading to the guillotine]. Before you make your decision, you need to understand we won't start with you. First, we start with your two-year old daughter, then your three sons, followed by your wife, before you. This is your final opportunity to step out of line, deny Him, and avoid death. What is your decision?"

The time to make our decision is now. Decide NOW NOT TO TAKE THE MARK, NO MATTER WHAT!

My wife and I have already discussed it. If this were to happen to my family, I would turn to my daughter, get on my knees and look her into her eyes and say, "I don't want you to fight them. Go up and lay down and do as they tell you. You won't feel a thing and in just a few minutes your brothers, your mother, and I will be with you!"

Patrick Henry said when confronted with denying his nation, "I regret that I only have one life to give for my country!" We should be prepared to say, "I regret that I have but one life to give for my Lord and Savior!" Jesus died for us. We should be prepared to die for Him! Most people alive today WILL have the opportunity to deny Jesus or die for Him!

Remember the Martyr's blessing. It is said that the blessing of being a Martyr is no pain when dying for Jesus. Ken Peters said, "The second the Scimitar sword touched my neck I was gone. I never felt a thing!" In reading **_"Foxe's Book of Martyrs,"_** Christians being burned at the stake, as the fire would burn the ropes from their hands, they would lift their arms praising God! They felt no pain!

WILL JESUS FORGIVE ME IF I TAKE THE MARK OF THE BEAST TO LIVE OR SO MY CHILDREN CAN EAT? NO! NO! NO! A THOUSAND TIMES, NO!

To take the Mark is to accept the wicked one and reject the kindness and love of Jesus.

The Mark will be a permanent mark. We are pretty sure it is not removable, but even if it is, even if you cut your hand off, you can't get your salvation back. You CAN'T BE FORGIVEN for taking the Mark of the Beast! It is the biggest mistake any person can make!

Some people have thought, "Jesus is love, he would never expect me or my children to starve for him!" Wrong! He has told his people in the past to die for Him. It still stands today. He died for all mankind. We should be willing to do die for Him. Jesus wants us to be willing to suffer for Him.

> *REV 2:8-10, ...Fear none of those things which thou shalt suffer: behold, the devil shall cast some of you into prison, that ye may be tried; and ye shall have tribulation ten days: BE THOU FAITHFUL UNTO DEATH, AND I WILL GIVE THEE A CROWN OF LIFE.*

> *REV 2:12-13, ...HOLDEST FAST MY NAME, and hast NOT DENIED MY FAITH, even in those days wherein Antipas was my faithful martyr, who was slain among you, where Satan dwelleth.*

Jesus wants us to be willing to die for Him! That goes against the spirit of the rapture protecting anyone. There are some things He will NOT forgive, and accepting the Beast is one of them.

Throughout all human history there are only three groups.

1. Those people IN the Book of Life who live forever.

2. Those NOT in the Book of Life who are tossed into the lake of fire which is body and soul death.

3. Those people who JOIN the Beast, the False Prophet, Lucifer in perdition, or the Fire Brimstone without soul-death.

If you take the Mark of the Beast you can cut your hand off, chisel it off your forehead, but you will not go to heaven. I'm just the messenger. I'm just showing you what the Word says.

THE SCARIEST VERSES IN REVELATION

REV 13:5-9, And there was given unto him [the Beast] *a mouth speaking great things and blasphemies;* [God gives him the most powerful oratory in human history. He will be the greatest speaker of all time.] *and power was given unto him to continue forty and two months.* [He is allowed to continue for 1,260 days, or three and one-half years which is 42 months.] *And he opened his mouth in blasphemy against God, to blaspheme his name, and his tabernacle, and them that dwell in heaven.* [He attacks all that is God, the Bible, those written in the Bible and most especially Jesus and his testimony.] *And it was given unto him to make war with the saints, and to overcome them: and power was given him over all kindreds, and tongues, and nations.* [He was just given the greatest oratory in history so we know this war against the saints is a war of words, but rest assured bullets will be the conclusion of it.] *And all that dwell upon the earth shall worship him, whose names are not written in the book of life of the Lamb slain from the foundation of the world.* [Only those whose names were written in the Book of life before the creation will resist! Most will fall.] *If any man have an ear, let him hear.*

Here are the scariest two verses in the Book of Revelation. Many Saints have guns and are quite capable of defending themselves and their families. Yet, these two verses are saying we are NOT to fight back against the Beast and his followers!

REV 13:10-11, He that leadeth into captivity shall go into captivity: he that killeth with the sword must be killed with the sword. Here is the patience and the faith of the saints.

The definition of "patience" in Revelation is different than in our world today. Revelation defines "patience" as: don't quit, don't give in, don't give up, hold on, and don't walk away from Jesus!

In layman's terms, this is saying the Beast will be given a special ability to defeat any and all humans with his words. Almost all humans WILL fall to the Beast. The believers must not kill the followers of the Beast. Our only option will be to run and hide. The following vision says most Christians WILL be found and killed.

CALL TO KILL CHRISTIANS AS "UNBELIEVERS"
Vision given to Prophet David Phillips

"Please understand that I am sharing to the best of my memory, as I was a relatively new believer in Jesus

Christ at the time and had never experienced anything like this before. This was an open vision while I was awake.

"I was in a church (Catholic at the time). During the service they called everybody to stand. When I stood up a vision immediately began. In the vision I saw what looked like a movie screen directly in front of me. Then, the left and right sides of the screen expanded at the same time to what looked like forever. Also, the top and bottom of the movie screen expanded to what looked like forever. I was no longer thinking about the church service. All I saw, or was thinking about, was the vision in front of me as it played.

"The vision that I saw was of a new Pope. The Pope that I saw was standing in front of great masses of people in Italy, at the Vatican. He was high so that he could speak to the people directly. There was great excitement in the crowd because of this Pope, because the Papacy had finally returned to Italy. He looked younger than past Popes- not frail. He was maybe in his 30's or 40's with dark hair and dark facial hair."

KEY POINT:

"What greatly troubled me were the words he was shouting. His words were not of love and kindness as with past Popes I had seen. He was threatening and attacking the Protestants, shouting that the true Church must rise up and unite against the Protestants. He was shouting that the Protestants are not true believers, but rather unbelievers. The crowd was shouting with rage and hatred in support of him and his words. He said the penalty for them must be death. The people were in complete agreement with this. They had been called to action, and the entire world would now rise in power to kill Protestants in all nations. The words he spoke were so frightening that I cannot explain how mere words can be so powerful in developing a reaction in you. It was unlike anything I had ever witnessed before.

"Somehow, I knew in my heart that he was talking about killing us– the true believers, who are far fewer in number. I knew that what he was saying was the opposite of the truth, but the people believed him. I thought, **BUT WE ARE THE TRUE BELIEVERS!** Life on earth had changed forever! **I thought: We will now be hunted and killed for our faith around the world. I am not ready for this!!!!!**

"All of a sudden, the screens came in and the vision ended. I was standing back in the Church, sweating from the vision. I did not know how long the vision lasted. I was so thankful that I was back at that church because persecution of the true believers had not yet started. At this time Pope John Paul II was still alive.

"I was made to know that our only option is to run and hide, but they will discover that when all the world has turned to the Beast there is nowhere. They will find you. Our only hope is to trust Jesus with our death."

~David Phillips

Jeremiah and Isaiah were shown believers were hiding in the days just before the return of Jesus.

JER 16:16, Behold, I will send for many fishers, saith the LORD, and they shall fish them; and after will I send for many hunters, and THEY SHALL HUNT THEM from every mountain, and from every hill, and OUT OF THE HOLES OF THE ROCKS.

I told you, you wouldn't like it. I don't like it either, but this is the plan and direction of Jesus. Run and hide from the Beast and his people but don't kill them! Eeeek! Knowing that the whole world is searching for Christians, and most will be found. This is serious information here! It's not entertainment.

The Bible is saying this guy is going to stand up and have a mouth which will convince everybody whose name is not in the Book of Life to take the Mark of the Beast!

America has probably fallen by this time, as leader of the world. The Beast will convince the sinners they are the true believers and should go out and kill the unbelievers [Saints]. He doesn't have to convince everybody to take the Mark. He just convinces enough non-Christians to go out kill the Christians, the ones that won't accept him. I heard it once said that if all Christians in America decided to go to church Sunday morning, only 5% could even get into a building! Meaning there's very few people that are really Christians.

God is going to send the Beast who is "the strong delusion." The Beast will have many deceptions so all who have not come to the knowledge of the truth– that Jesus is God would believe a lie. What lie? The lie. The lie that the Beast is the Messiah to the Jews and Christians, the Vishnu to the Hindu, and the Mahdi to the Muslims! Most every religion is looking for their great leader or savior to return! The Beast will be their god they look for! It is important to read all this scripture.

2TH 2:1-12 Now we beseech you, brethren, by the coming of our Lord Jesus Christ, and by our gathering together unto him, That ye be not soon shaken in mind, or be troubled, neither by spirit, nor by word, nor by letter as from us, as that the day of Christ is at hand. Let no man deceive you by any means: for that day shall not come, except there come A FALLING AWAY FIRST, and that man of sin be revealed, the son of perdition; Who opposeth and exalteth himself above all that is called God, or that is worshipped; so that HE AS GOD SITTETH IN THE TEMPLE OF GOD, SHEWING HIMSELF THAT HE IS GOD. 9 Even him, whose coming is after the working of Satan with all power and signs and lying wonders, ...because they received not the love of the truth, that they might be saved. And for this cause GOD SHALL SEND THEM STRONG DELUSION, THAT THEY SHOULD BELIEVE A LIE: THAT THEY ALL MIGHT BE DAMNED WHO BELIEVED NOT THE TRUTH, but had pleasure in unrighteousness.

Chapter 4

World Government

After America is defeated by the Russians, all the world will be terrified and consider capitalism defeated because America fell. They form a new world government. The Beast rises to total power over it. This is a vision John, in Revelation 13, was shown of the rise of the world government. The Bible speaks of a world government in several places, but these verses are probably the most complete description of the forming of world government in the Bible.

REV 13:1-8, And I stood upon the sand of the sea, [People] *and saw a beast* [World government] *rise up out of the sea,* [Worldly people] *having seven heads* [Seven continents] *and ten horns,* [Divided into 10 global regions] *and upon his horns ten crowns,* [Each region has a regional ruler] *and upon his heads the name of blasphemy.* [Each ruler blasphemes which means they attack God.]

2 And the beast [World government] *which I saw was like unto a leopard,* [Muslim] *and his feet were as the feet of a bear,* [Russian] *and his mouth as the mouth of a lion:* [English] *and the dragon* [Satan] *gave him his power, and his seat, and great authority.*

3 And I saw one of his heads [A regional ruler which is the Beast] *as it were wounded to death; and his deadly wound was healed: and all the world wondered after the beast.* [All the world is amazed when one of these regional rulers dies or appears to die but comes back to life. They will say, "This is God."]

4 And they worshipped the dragon [If you worship the Beast you worship the Devil.] *which gave power unto the beast: and they worshipped the beast, saying, Who is like unto the beast? who is able to make war with him?* [Who can defeat one who returns from the dead?]

5 And there was given unto him a mouth speaking great [Bad] *things and blasphemies;* [This is a test from God upon all those who dwell on earth. God gives the Beast the ability to speak with great power and he uses it to speak against all that is holy.] *and power was given unto him to continue forty and two months.* [The Tribulation is seven years long or 2,560 days. The Beast is allowed to rule the earth for the last half which is 1,260 days or 42 months.]

6 And he opened his mouth in blasphemy [Attacks God.] *against God, to blaspheme his name, and his tabernacle, and them that dwell in heaven.* [All that is Christian will be attacked.]

7 And it was given unto him to make war with the saints, and to overcome them: [Satan is allowed to test all people especially the Christians. God allows him to defeat the saints. The Beast defeats them with his words. Once defeated all the Christians must stand for Christ or fall for the Beast.] *and power was given him over all kindreds, and tongues, and nations.*

8 And all that dwell upon the earth shall worship him, whose names are not written in the book of life of the Lamb slain from the foundation of the world. [All people on earth will be forced to take the Mark, worship the Beast, his image or receive the number of his name or be killed, and most people will! If your name is in the Book of Life you will continue to resist the Beast. But for you to resist you must accept Jesus BEFORE YOU SEE AND/OR HEAR THE BEAST! Once you hear him if you have not already asked Jesus to be your God you will be so struck with him you will accept him as God and be damned! Many will be beheaded REV 20:4.]

*REV 17:8, The beast that thou sawest was, and is not; and shall ascend out of the bottomless pit, and go into perdition: and THEY THAT DWELL ON THE EARTH SHALL **WONDER**,* [Marvel or admire] *WHOSE NAMES WERE NOT WRITTEN IN THE BOOK OF LIFE FROM THE FOUN-DATION OF THE WORLD, WHEN THEY BEHOLD THE BEAST THAT WAS, AND IS NOT, AND YET IS.*

REV 13:10, HE THAT LEADETH INTO CAPTIVITY SHALL GO INTO CAP-TIVITY: HE THAT KILLETH WITH THE SWORD MUST BE KILLED WITH THE SWORD. [Christians should not fight against those in the New World Order!] *Here is the patience and the faith of the saints.* [Don't turn people over to the New World Order government or you will be turned over, and don't kill them or you will be killed is a direct warning to Christians.]

REV 13:11-18, And I beheld an-other beast [The rise of the Cath-olic Church.] *coming up out of the earth; and he had two horns like a lamb,* [There are two leaders in the Catholic Church] *and he spake as a dragon.* [The dragon is the devil. This is the second beast commonly referred to as the False Prophet. He will hijack the Catholic Church and become the leader. He will sound like a man of God but will be saying what the devil tells him to say.]

12 And he exerciseth all the power of the first beast [Antichrist] *before him, and causeth the earth and them which dwell therein to worship the first beast, whose deadly wound was healed.* [He commands all the earth to make an image which will prob-ably be some sort of clone linked to the new a global 5G computer network who commands all people to worship the image or be killed.]

13 And he doeth great wonders, [Beware of lying signs and wonders which will deceive.] *so that he ma-keth fire come down from heaven on the earth in the sight of men,*

14 And deceiveth them that dwell on the earth by the means of those mira-cles which he had power to do in the sight of the beast; saying to them that dwell on the earth, that they should make an image to the beast, [clone?] *which had the wound by a sword, and did live.* [He uses miracles like calling lightening or lasers to come out of the sky to prove he is God.]

15 And he had power to give life unto the image of the beast, that the image of the beast should both speak, and cause that as many as would not worship the image of the beast should be killed.

16 And he causeth all, both small and great, rich and poor, free and bond, to receive a mark in their right hand, or in their foreheads: [The False Prophet commands all people on earth to accept the Beast as the new "Man-God" or be killed. He will probably command all who follow the Beast to kill those who do not.]

17 And that no man might buy or sell, save he that had the mark, or the name of the beast, or the number of his name. [Probably our cell phones linked to the 5G global Internet. You have to take the Mark in order to log on. If you can't log on you can't buy or sell. Part of the log on process is taking the Mark.]

18 Here is wisdom. Let him that hath understanding count the number of the beast: for it is the number of a man; and his number is Six hundred threescore and six [666].

REV 17:17, For God hath put in their hearts to fulfil his will, and to agree, and GIVE THEIR KINGDOM UNTO THE BEAST, until the words of God shall be fulfilled. [When the world government is formed all national borders will be removed.]

All nations will give all their wealth, including all their military weapons, to the Beast.

All people on earth will have to swear allegiance to the Beast. As a sign of their obedience, they will receive the Mark or the number of his name. Even worshiping, bending the knee, taking an oath to the Beast, or his image will still remove your eternal life.

Many years ago, it was thought that those who resist would be sent to re-ed-ucation camps. Not so! The scriptures say they will simply be killed.

REV 6:11, And white robes were given unto every one of them; and it was said unto them, that they should rest yet for a little season, until their fellow servants also and their brethren, that SHOULD BE KILLED as they were, should be fulfilled.

REV 13:15, And he had power to give life unto the image of the beast, that the image of the beast should both speak, and CAUSE THAT AS MANY AS WOULD NOT WORSHIP THE IMAGE OF THE BEAST SHOULD BE KILLED.

THE LAST THREE SUPERPOWERS FORMED BEFORE THE WORLD GOVERNMENT

DAN 7:2-11, Daniel spake and said, I saw in my vision by night, and, behold, the four winds of the heaven strove upon the great sea. And four great beasts [Four superpowers] *came up from the sea,* [People] *diverse one from another.*

4 The first was like a lion, [England] *and had eagle's wings:* [America] *I beheld till the wings thereof were plucked,* [Christians moved from England and God formed America.] *and it was lifted up from the earth, and made stand upon the feet as a man, and a man's heart was given to it.* [America was formed.]

5 And behold another beast, a second, like to a bear, [Russia] *and it raised up itself on one side,* [Russia's strength is on her West side.] *and it had three ribs in the mouth of it between the teeth of it: and they said thus unto it, Arise, devour much flesh.*

6 After this I beheld, and lo another, like a leopard, [Muslims] *which had upon the back of it four wings* [Caliphate of four nations.] *of a fowl; the beast had also four heads;* [Each nation has one leader.] *and dominion was given to it.*

7 After this I saw in the night visions, and behold a fourth beast, [World government.] *dreadful and terrible, and strong exceedingly; and it had great iron teeth: it devoured and brake in pieces, and stamped the residue with the feet of it: and it was diverse from all the beasts that were before it; and it had ten horns.* [Seven continents divided into ten global regions.]

8 I considered the horns, and, behold, there came up among them another little horn, [The Beast/Antichrist.] *before whom there were three of the first horns plucked up by the roots:* [In his rise to power he destroys three other global regional leaders.] *and, behold, in this horn were eyes like the eyes of man,* [He is a man.] *and a mouth speaking great things.* [God gives him skill in speaking great (bad) things against all that is holy.]

When Jesus returns he destroys all kingdoms on earth and sets up his eternal Kingdom.

9 I BEHELD TILL THE THRONES WERE CAST DOWN, [Jesus returns and sets up an everlasting Kingdom.]

11 I beheld then because of THE VOICE OF THE GREAT WORDS WHICH THE HORN SPAKE: I beheld even TILL THE BEAST WAS SLAIN, [Jesus destroys the tares with the Morning Star light sword from the mouth of Jesus.] *AND HIS BODY DESTROYED, AND GIV-*

EN TO THE BURNING FLAME. [Tossed into the Lake of fire and tormented forever Rev. 20:10].

This is the return
Of Jesus on Trumpets
At Armageddon, the final war
Between the Beast and Jesus.

REV 19:19-21, And I saw THE BEAST, and the kings of the earth, and their ARMIES, GATHERED TOGETHER TO MAKE WAR against him that sat on the horse, and against his army. And the beast was taken, and with him the false prophet that wrought miracles before him, with which he deceived them that had received the mark of the beast, and them that worshipped his image. These both were cast alive into a lake of fire burning with brimstone. And the remnant were slain with the sword [Morning Star] *of him that sat upon the horse, which sword proceeded out of his mouth: and all the fowls were filled with their flesh.*

The Interpretation
By Daniel to the King:

DAN 7:14-27, And there was given him [Jesus] *dominion,* [An empire.] *and glory, and a kingdom, that all people, nations, and languages, should serve him: his dominion is an EVERLASTING DOMINION, which shall not pass away, and his kingdom that which shall not be destroyed. These great beasts, which are four, are four kings,* [Superpowers] *which shall arise out of the earth. But the saints of the most High shall take the kingdom, and possess the kingdom for ever, even for ever and ever. Then I would know the truth of the FOURTH BEAST,* [The Beast] *which was diverse from all the others, exceeding dreadful, whose teeth were of iron,* [Roman empire/European Union] *and his nails of brass;* [Grecian empire] *which devoured, brake in pieces, and stamped the residue with his feet;* [Conquers the whole world.] *And of the ten horns that were in his head,* [ten nations] *and of the other which came up, and before whom three fell; even of that horn that had eyes, AND A MOUTH THAT SPAKE VERY GREAT THINGS,* [Attacks the Bible, God, Jesus and all that is Christian even all other religions.] *whose look was more stout than his fellows.* [The Beast will be the most attractive man on earth.] *I beheld, and the same horn made WAR WITH THE SAINTS, and prevailed against them;* [Destroys the belief of many including many lukewarm Christians and kills those refusing to take the Mark.] *Until the Ancient of days came, and judgment was given to the saints of the most High; and the time came that the saints possessed the kingdom. Thus he said, The fourth beast shall be the fourth kingdom upon earth, which shall be diverse from all kingdoms, and shall devour the whole earth, and shall TREAD IT DOWN, AND BREAK IT IN PIECES. And the ten horns out of this kingdom are ten kings that shall arise: AND ANOTHER SHALL RISE AFTER THEM;* [The Beast is not recognized until he overthrows three other regional rulers.] *AND HE SHALL BE DIVERSE FROM THE FIRST, AND HE SHALL SUBDUE THREE KINGS. And he shall speak great words against the most High, and shall wear out the saints of the most High, and think to change times and laws: and they shall be given into his hand until a time and times and the dividing of time.* [The Tribulation is seven years long but the Beast is in full control

for the last three and one-half years. Which is 42 months also stated as time, [one year] times [two years] and the dividing of time. [total 3½ years] *But the judgment shall sit, and they shall take away his* [The Beast's] *dominion, to consume and to destroy it unto the end. And the kingdom and dominion, and the greatness of the kingdom under the whole heaven, shall be given to the people of the saints of the most High, whose kingdom is an everlasting kingdom, and all dominions shall serve and obey him.*

Terry Bennett says the angel Gabriel came and laid out three 7-year time frames to him. For five days, beginning December 10, 2001, Gabriel came and showed him much of the future. He laid out the future in three sets of seven-year time frames and has visited him several times since then.

He says Gabriel visited with him for several hours each day and told him what would occur during a 21-year period starting in 2008 through 2028. He divided the period into three seven-year periods. He then spoke about each seven-year period revealing what would be the predominant issue of each period. As Gabriel spoke about these things, Terry was shown visions allowing him to see the events happening.

Each period will have a predominant issue beginning with economic trouble, then governmental changes, and finally the rise of a one-world religion. In all of the 21 years (from 2008-2028), there will be some elements from all three of these areas. [But Prophets Sundar Selvaraj and Maurice Sklar said that a delay has been given.]

This is part of what Prophet Terry Bennett says he was told concerning the Beast:

"There will arise a new government in Europe, Gabriel warned me, "Keep your eyes on four nations. They are signposts to what is coming. Keep your eyes on Greece, Italy, Spain and France. Greece is going to want another Alexander the Great. Italy is going to want and emperor. Spain is going to want a king and queen. France is going to want another Napoleon. Satan is going to offer all three to them in one person. They will say yes. Through chaos they will gain control."

~Terry Bennett

The chaos will be created, purposeful, while other chaotic events will come because once they get chaos going, they will be unable to control it. The economic chaos will lead to dramatic governmental change in Europe, and in our nation. It will begin in the economic arena and then go forth into the governmental arena. Major governmental changes are going to happen in various parts of the world, particularly in Europe.

WHAT IS THE TRIBULATION?

The word "Tribulation" means trouble or pressure, but in the context of Bible prophecy the Tribulation is speaking of the last seven years before the end of the old heaven and old earth on the day of Trumpets when Jesus returns. Of the 6,000 years since Adam and Eve, the first humans, this will be the worst time in all human history.

Jesus said that unless He returned no flesh would be saved. So, mankind approaches near total annihilation before He returns [Matthew 24:22]. You may ask why? Why would a loving God bring such devastation upon all that live on the earth?

Two reasons:

1. Jesus is the righteous Judge. He set forth the laws by which mankind lives. It is as simple as this. He blesses those who follow them, and curses those who don't. He blesses and curses to the exact degree of their obedience or disobedience. Those who do His will are blessed. As the earth became evil, their punishment increases. The earth has become so evil almost all people deserve death.

2. This world was never intended to be eternal. This earth and life is temporary, only a test to see how we follow God's laws to determine our admittance to the Kingdom of Heaven and our level of blessings throughout eternity. Many people who decided to follow Jesus, did so in a low moment of their life. They tried to be happy in their own strength and failed. They finally decided to follow Jesus. Difficulty gets people searching for answers and in their search, many receive Jesus.

If Jesus were to return with no difficulty more people would be lost. By Jesus sending hard times, it will cause millions more to be saved from wrath and receive eternal life.

Jesus is trying to get even the most hardened criminal to repent and ask forgiveness so they can have eternal life! The seven-year Tribulation is God, in his infinite wisdom removing life's comforts, causing people to turn to him thus more people will live eternally.

The trouble starts with storms, tornadoes, hurricanes, financial collapses and the fall of governments. But it gets increasingly worse, changing to earthquakes, wars, meteors, and tsunamis. It concludes in the last week with the sea, rivers, and all the water on earth turning to undrinkable blood. The sun novae's and gets seven times hotter [Isaiah 30:26] then goes out! The greatest earthquake in human history, levels every mountain and fills in every valley and the sea!

The temperature of space is -455F degrees. When the sun goes out within 48 hours, the earth starts to freeze causing the atmosphere to release all moisture forming 75-pound hail about 3 to 7 foot-deep around the earth [REV 11:19, 16:21]. Jesus uses the Morning Star light-sword to burn those who took the Mark. The Morning Star turns them to ashes! No kidding. Read Revelation, chapters 16 and 19.

THE GOOD NEWS!

The good news is you can know for certain that when you die you will be given eternal life! You will never die, nor sorrow, nor hunger, nor have any pain! You can't purchase it or earn it. Eternal life is a free gift. It is not easy, but it is free.

JOH 3:16, For God so loved the world, that he gave his only begotten Son, that whosoever believeth in him should NOT PERISH, but have everlasting life.

ROM 3:23, For ALL HAVE SINNED, and come short of the glory of God;

EPH 2:8, For by grace are ye saved through faith; and that not of yourselves: IT IS THE GIFT OF GOD: NOT OF WORKS, lest any man should boast.

ROM 10:9, That if thou shalt CONFESS WITH THY MOUTH THE LORD JESUS, and SHALT BELIEVE IN THINE HEART THAT GOD HATH RAISED HIM FROM THE DEAD, THOU SHALT BE SAVED. For WITH THE HEART MAN believeth unto righteousness; and with the MOUTH CONFESSION IS MADE UNTO SALVATION.

ACT 2:38, Then Peter said unto them, REPENT, AND BE BAPTIZED EVERY ONE OF YOU IN THE NAME OF JESUS CHRIST for the remission of sins, and ye shall receive the gift of the Holy Ghost.

If you would like to live forever in peace, joy, and happiness, pray this prayer out loud to Jesus:

*"**Dear Heavenly Father,***

I admit I am a sinner. I know I have made mistakes. Please forgive me. I confess with my mouth; and believe in my heart that Jesus IS THE CHRIST, the Son of the Living God who died on the cross, arose three days later. I receive his sacrificed blood to wash my sins away, write my name in the Book of Life, keep me Holy and save me in the day of trouble.

In Jesus' Name, Amen."

Now you must go tell someone out loud that you have accepted Jesus as your Lord:

MAT 10:32-33 Whosoever therefore shall confess me before men, him will I confess also before my Father which is in heaven.

33 But whosoever shall deny me before men, him will I also deny before my Father which is in heaven.

Chapter 5

The Nine Greatest Deceptions in History!

Remember the Devil has been around since before mankind was created and he is exceedingly cunning, intelligent far beyond humans. He has a well-designed plan of deception so good it will trick ALMOST everyone on earth into worshiping him. The following are only a few of his tactics to avoid, he may use more. Be aware of them, don't be surprised, expect them and do not fall for the greatest deceptions in human history!

I first heard of them from a man I interviewed on the radio back in the early 1990's. He was speaking everywhere then he just disappeared. From daily radio shows to interviews the next day... then he was gone. Many people believe he was killed because he was exposing the darkest secrets of the devil on radio. To this day his body has never been found! So, I know what I am revealing is serious! I know it is true not because the man was killed, I know it is true because I found verification in the scriptures of Truth.

When I started writing this book the secrets that man revealed came back to me. In my opinion, it was the Lord hinting to include them in this book. Most of these deceptions are revealed in the prophecies although veiled. Those not in the prophecies are in today's news!

I changed the wording by bringing the same point to light straight from the Bible. He made several points I would not have seen, so Lord bless him! I'm about to expose the devil's biggest darkest plans to deceive mankind in the days of the Tribulation!

ARCHAEOLOGY DECEPTION:

Picture the fake news... CNN, the source of all the truth on the earth, NOT!– announces a great earthquake hit the earth! A great discovery was made! An underground chamber was discovered. And in this chamber, we found these tablets and we found this and that, and this ancient thing and that ancient artifact. In this box... and it was... it... here's what it is. This is what we found... . And uh, this guy [the Beast] he's really God!

The tablets say, "All of the Muslims were lied to. All of the Satanists you were lied to. All the Hindu's you were lied to. All of the Christians, you were all lied to. All that Jesus stuff is rubbish. Proof, we got it right here. You've been lied to. This man, or world leader is God!"

So much so that, "if it were possible it would deceive even the very elect."

Expect earthquakes to supposedly reveal new discoveries of ancient artifacts designed to destroy the foundations of all religions.

Expect to hear, "We have all been mistaken!" "We misunderstood." "We didn't have all the information." Don't be fooled.

Expect a wonderful plan so good over 95% of the humans on the planet will quickly accept it as proof beyond any reasonable doubt saying past beliefs and laws were based upon inaccurate or missing information. The news will report a great discovery of information, so convincing the earth will accept it as correct!

Expect the "new society" to correct "old errors" with "new revelations from the one true-God" "new laws and standards" so the world can finally live in peace [by peace he shall destroy many].

The Real Ark of the Covenant Has Been Discovered!

From 1989 to 1999, I was involved with the Full Gospel Business Men's Fellowship. A wonderful organization who helped me discover many wonderful gifts and blessings in the Lord. I am very thankful for this divine organization! Our chapter had invited Ron Wyatt to speak in Omaha, Nebraska.

At the speaking engagement, Ron showed a 90 minute video called ***"Presentation of Discoveries,"*** which is still available at ***https://wyattmuseum.com/shop/presentation-of-discoveries***.

Ron Wyatt's presentation displayed the evidences of Noah's Ark, Sodom & Gomorrah, the Red Sea crossing, Mt. Sinai, and the Ark of the Covenant; the complete overview of the discoveries. Ideal for sharing with groups.

In 1991, I received one of his newsletters that included an invitation for people to go on a tour to see these discoveries. I knew I didn't have the funds to go on this trip but I said to myself, "I am going on this tour!"

I recall walking into the bathroom, where my wife was at the time, showed her the newsletter, and pronounced, "I am going!" She took one look at it, and proclaimed, "I am going too!"

God, in His perfect will and plans, arranged for the money to come in and we both went on the tour. God also provided me with a VCR Recorder as a Christmas gift, which in those days was very expensive.

I wanted to make sure I caught every minute of what Ron Wyatt said, so I purchased about 15 high quality VHS tapes at a nice camera shop. At the time I thought it was all for my personal interest. I could never have dreamed the information would win "thousands upon thousands" to Christ!

The videos of the tour have been edited to one two-hour DVD, available at ***www.prophecyclub.com*** or instantly viewable online at ***www. WatchProphecyClub.com***. It is called, ***"Archaeology Confirms the Bible,"*** by Stan Johnson.

The short version of the tour is this. We went to what I believe is the real Noah's Ark. We walked all over the ark and I brought back a piece of what I unofficially believe was petrified wood. We saw its anchor stones, Gomorrah, the rock that Moses struck, giant bones of pre-flood people, the crossing site of the Red Sea, and the

Archaeological evidence at the Garden Tomb of Jesus at Golgotha. If you like the facts, this video is great to show in churches and homes.

The most important part of the tour was the information about the Ark of the Covenant. When the world sees the information regarding the Ark of the Covenant it will remove all doubt that this is the genuine Ark of the Covenant– and thus the Bible is true. When the world can see for themselves the hard evidence of the; three cross holes, the three signs, the crack, the blood in the crack, the blood on the cover of the ark, the cover cracked open allowing the blood through, and the blood on the west side of the Ark there will be no doubt!

The blood of the sacrificed Lambs was dripped on the east side of the Ark. The blood of Jesus dropped on the west side of the Ark.

LEV 16:14, And he shall take of the BLOOD of the bullock, and sprinkle it with his finger upon the mercy seat EASTWARD; and before the MERCY SEAT shall he sprinkle of the blood with his finger seven times.

Remember the Ark of the Covenant is a large chair made of wood overlaid with gold. It is the Throne of God on earth! The seat of the Ark is called the "Mercy Seat." Ron said he took a small scrapping of the dried blood on the WEST SIDE of the Mercy Seat and took it to a scientific laboratory requesting the blood be reconstituted. This means adding distilled water to it. He asked them to tell him what the substance was all the while refusing to tell them anything about it.

With all the evidence gathered by the scientist, they told Ron that it is human blood, but they were startled when they saw the somatids were still alive! The Blood of Jesus, almost 2,000 years old, was still alive! Why wouldn't it be? Jesus has the keys of hell and death. No one took His life, He laid down His life to redeem us all!

They looked at it under a very powerful microscope to discover it only had one set of Chromosomes! As you recall all human blood has 23 Chromosomes from the Father and 23 from the Mother. The X or Y determines male or female. This blood only had ONE SET OF CHROMOSOMES! This proves Jesus was literally the Son of God.

Ron said one time when he was doing some work in the chamber where the ark was located, an angel appeared and told him that when the Beast comes out with his secular "Ten Commandments" and/or requires people to take the Mark of the Beast, the discovery of the Ark of the Covenant will be revealed to the world to show them the truth!

Ron said they have video showing the three cut-out cross-holes, the crack to the left of the center cross-hole, the blood running down the crack that dripped on the Ark of the Covenant, the Throne of God on earth, the microscopic video footage showing the somatids are alive, and only one set of Chromosomes that prove beyond any reasonable doubt that Jesus is the Christ, the Messiah, the Lamb of God!

MAT 1:20, But while he thought on these things, behold, the angel of the

Lord appeared unto him in a dream, saying, Joseph, thou son of David, fear not to take unto thee Mary thy wife: for THAT WHICH IS CONCEIVED IN HER IS OF THE HOLY GHOST.

You see the Holy Ghost was the Father of Jesus in that this blood only has one set of Chromosomes thereby proves this was the Blood of Jesus! It not only proves the Bible is true, but it proves the greatest of all truths that Jesus truly is God!

To fulfill the Levitical commandments of sacrifice, the blood of the Lamb had to be sprinkled on the Mercy Seat. God arranged for the blood of only one human in history to drip on the Ark of the Covenant, the blood of Jesus the Messiah, Lamb of God.

RON WYATT DISCOVERS THE ARK OF THE COVENANT:

This is Ron's Wyatt's testimony given in 1991 in Israel on our tour. We were at the Garden Tomb. After this talk, we visited the tomb where he showed us the Archaeological evidence that would convince even the skeptic that this was the place Jesus was crucified, where His blood had dripped on the Ark of the Covenant, and where He was subsequently buried.

Having been a public speaking instructor for 13 years, having heard and commented on thousands of talks, I can spot a talk that is made up as opposed to a person telling an incident that really happened. It is easy once you know what to look for.

When a person has made up a story they stand still and just speak. If they were, for example, telling a story

of riding a bike, hitting a stone causing a crash, there would be no actions to match the story because it didn't really happen. However, when the incident really happened, we would see a person hold their hands in a position as if they had them on the handlebars. As they talked, they would look down and their hands would jerk to the side illustrating they hit the rock. These actions are never there when it is a story made up, but on the other hand, they are never missing when the person is reliving the incident.

For those that haven't seen it yet, I observed those kinds of movements as Ron talked. I am totally convinced that Ron was telling the truth when he tells us that he discovered the Ark of the Covenant.

As he talked, when he pointed at a dump, I saw his left arm go out. Throughout his talk these kinds of movements accompanied Ron's talk. You can trust this talk.

It is very important that you see the story of Ron's talk, entitled, ***"Archaeology Confirms the Bible,"*** by Stan Johnson. It can be viewed at ***WatchProphecyClub.com***. There are three versions so be sure and watch the one by Stan Johnson. This talk begins at the 1:07.30 time-code. I am totally convinced Ron is telling the truth when he tells us he discovered the Ark of the Covenant.

I personally recorded Ron's talk in the seating area of the Garden Tomb in Israel in 1991. This is a transcription of that talk:

Ron Wyatt Testimony:

"One Day I was walking along this escarpment with an archaeologist friend of mine, and those of you who know me, I am not given to salubrious soliloquies, I am hard headed, hard-nosed and I want to know the facts, and that's all I want to know.

"But as I was walking by, my left arm pointed to a dump under the wall of the escarpment, and my mouth said "That's Jeremiah's grotto and the Ark of the Covenant is in there.

"Well, I love the Israelis, but they are not overly generous, and I think our friend [our Israeli guide] here will agree, but this man said, "That's wonderful. We will let you excavate; we will give you a place to stay, we will give you all the help you need, we will provide your food and we will do your laundry.

"How many times has an Israeli offered that to a *Goyim*? Not often. [A term used by a Jew to refer to someone who is not Jewish.]

"So anyway, I was flabbergasted, I had not even thought about the Ark of the Covenant, or Jeremiah's cave or none of that stuff. I said later, I will do this, but now I have got to go home. So, I went home, and I dug through History books [to discover why the Ark of the Covenant might be there.]

"I found out that Jerusalem at the time of the vanishing of the Ark of the Covenant and the other major furnishings of the first Temple, when they vanished, the city was surrounded by a siege wall. II Kings 25th chapter– Nebuchadnezzar has forts against

the city roundabout, and the Hebrew simply means "Siege Wall." Titus did the same thing. Part of Titus' wall has survived to the North. They were built out of range of the catapults in the city. The "catapult-ology" had not advanced since Nebuchadnezzar's time and the Roman catapults in that period of time had about the same range as the one in Nebuchadnezzar's time. So, we can conclude that Nebuchadnezzar's wall was about where Titus' wall was.

"Now the Ark of the Covenant vanished out of this besieged city. Some people say it was taken to Mount Horeb, some people say that Solomon's son by the Queen of Shiba snookered him into making a replica and he traded. But the Shekinah Glory didn't leave until about 586bc. This man might have snookered Solomon and everybody else around, but he could not snooker the Shekinah Glory. So that did not happen.

"Now then, the only place short of God blinding part of the Babylonian Army and having some of His people take this out and hide it, was that it had to be hidden in the city, or inside the siege wall. The city is being systematically excavated down underneath the tunnels, the caves and everything, with very scientific methods. I went to the Israeli Archaeological Authorities, including the gentleman I was speaking with when my mouth said something that my brain, shall we say didn't go along with, or had no idea about, and I explained how it had to be in one of these, inside that siege wall. I thought that it was there from my research.

Ron is Permitted to Dig:

"So, they gave me a permit based on that and we started digging. As we dug, we found cut outs in the cliff face where three public signs related to the crucifixion were setup when a well-known criminal was to be crucified. Now, this arrangement, I always thought, was just for Christ. It was not. This is how the Romans did it, and they had captured Barabbas who had stirred up a lot of trouble in the area– rebelled and tried to overthrow the government, he didn't have a lot of luck, but he tried it, and so he was sentenced to be crucified. He was to be crucified in a very public manner. Now, some say "On a hill far away." This is a hill far away, it's a little below the crest because they made a quarry through here, but it's still on Mount Moriah.

The Crucifixion Site:

"Now then, they always crucified people right along the side of a very busy road where the most people will see. They crucified, because it was meant to intimidate anybody who would be thinking about trying something. They put the name of the person and what they were accused of in the chief local languages. In Jerusalem it was Hebrew, Greek and Latin (or Roman) and there's three cutouts there. In other cities they put up whatever languages were used there, but Roman was always one of those languages.

"As we excavated down the escarpment and found these cutouts. The wall that was on the outside, away from the cliff face got so high and unstable

that we decided to sink a shaft down, to see what strata we would find. We did this and we turned the samples in appropriately. We did carbon-14 dating on the chard wood that we found at different levels, we turned in the mortars and pestles, and the last one I handed in they said, "This is ten thousand years old." Jebusite of course, but anyway, when we got down to the bottom we came back up to where the ledge of the cliff (it had been cut down into) It's called the Roman level, it was at the top of this thing and everything below that was pre-Roman. We went along in a horizontal shaft along the cliff face, carefully documenting everything as we went. Any archaeologist that doesn't do this, is a criminal because people deserve to know what happened here and what was found. Not just some made up story, not some things that were carried in from another dig and put here so they could say, "Well we find this here, this proves such and such." There's a lot of that goes on and in school they teach you, you do not go out and dig to see what is there, you decide what is there and then you see to it that that's what you find. This is what they teach in school. So anyway, we went along this wall at the Roman level. We found Roman coins, we found Roman glass, we found Roman pottery– all this stuff we turned all of this in. It's in boxes over in the basement in storage at the Rockefeller Museum.

"As we went along, I found this cut out rock, and I thought "Man, that's unusual." So, I picked the thing up and I noticed there was a depression under there. So, I started digging careful-ly down through there, and it was just some debris, but it was a cross hole filled with debris. Apparently when these cross holes were not in use for cru-cifixion, they had plugs they put in them so horses or people walking by wouldn't break a leg and so they wouldn't fill up and then have to clean them every time they were going to use them. I was told to put that in a safe place which I did. It's still in a safe place. [It can be viewed at the Ron Wyatt Museum.]

"It dawned upon me that this had to be where Christ was crucified be-cause this was twelve feet below these cutouts in the cliff face and it was at the Roman level because we found the coins of Tiberius and some others we know that was open to the public for several years including the point in time when Christ was crucified. As we were working there, we noticed a crack in the cliff right by the left side where this cross hole was. Well that didn't mean a lot because this thing has been fractured considerably and if you look along this escarpment there is a lot of cracks in there and the Bible says that when Christ died there was an earth-quake and the rocks were rent. Today I know that that crack occurred at that moment in time, then I didn't know that. What was I excavating for? What was I looking for? What was my per-mit about? It was to see if the Ark of the Covenant had been hidden in this escarpment, and I had people I had to report to periodically.

"I was running out of money and it was time to go home and I prayed, "Lord, what shall I do?" I was im-pressed to break right through the cliff face and that seemed very ignorant to me so I kept looking around and I found some very old buildings, old foundations, old alter stones which I left in place as any good archaeologist would do. When we got ready to go, the day before we were to fly out, my oldest son (it was his turn in the hole) and we were passing our tools out to store them and he said "Dad you al-ways pray about things. Why haven't you prayed about this, so you'll know where to dig?" and I said, "I have," and he said, "Well, what happened?" and I said, "I was impressed to break through this wall." He asked, "Why don't I do it– I have done dumber things than that before." I said ok and had him holler up at my younger son to pass the tools back down.

"Here this crack was in the cliff face that went right by the left side of the wall and I decided if I made my chis-el crack over here that I could just pop this out. Then I would have a nice piece that I could put back and wouldn't damage anything. And so, we did this, we popped this out and way back in the little back end of that crack was a dark hole. I said, "Give me the flashlight." So, I shined it back in there and here was this cave chamber. Well I thought the Ark of the Covenant has got to be sitting right back there and I went of into "never-never land." I mean goose-bumps, the whole bit.

Ark Discovered
January 6, 1982, 2 P.M.

"We quickly enlarged the hole and got in. Well, the Ark of the Covenant wasn't sitting there, so I worked and worked and poked around in this little hole and that little hole and followed this erosion path through the limestone. Finally, the 6th of January, 1982 at two o'clock in the afternoon (something else an archaeologist always does when you enter a chamber where you think something may be, you look at your watch and you make a note of that. It may be important. If you don't find anything in there you can forget about it, but you should look). So, I did that. I went in there. Nothing but rocks.

"Ordinarily I would have crawled right back out of that place, but my sons had gotten double pneumonia. They were running fevers of about a hundred and four, and so was I. I sent them home and I decided that I was either going to find that this trip, or die in the hole! I really did. That's not very bright, but if you're sick enough it seemed very logical to me.

"I got this little Arab guy. He wasn't very big, and he was marvelous at getting into places and shining the light around so I could see if they were empty or if they had anything in there. We want along like this and we came to a little hole where the water had eroded a bit through there and there was a stalactite (1:21:10) hanging right down over the hole. So, I took my hammer and I carefully tapped at the base and laid it aside so that we could have that for future reference if necessary. Then I made the hole big enough or him to get in and this is the way we had been working.

"He crawls in there and I start to hand the light back in there to him and here he came out terrified! Absolutely terrified! If I hadn't gotten out of his way, I honestly believe he would have taken me apart getting out. It was mindless terror. That made me suspect that there was something special in there. He said "What's in there! What's in there. I'm not going back in there"! Well, that was fine by me and I made the hole big enough so that I could get in there and that is the only reason that I looked in that cave because it looked very unpromising. So, I crawled around on these rocks. The place was full of them. About eighteen inches of clearance to the ceiling and I shine my light down through the little openings down through the rocks. I saw a spot of gold here and I spot gold there, and my heart started pounding like you wouldn't believe! I started taking these rocks and sticking them here, there and everywhere. I actually ended up with rocks behind my shoulders and right there was a veneered table. I thought that's the table of showbread– later I found out by reading the book of Samuel a little more carefully that Solomon made ten more of them besides the one that Moses had Bezaleel make out in the wilderness. I didn't know if that was a copy or the real thing. At that point in time we didn't know that.

"I happened to notice this stone box right in front of me and the lid was cracked. I thought there has got to be something special in that box. I looked up to see what I can do to get rid of some more rocks and I saw some brown, dark brown stuff. I looked on up the wall and here it had come through a crack and down the wall and unto that broken area of that lid. Suddenly, it all came together. The cut outs. The cross hole. The crack. The Ark of the Covenant and Christ's Blood on the Mercy Seat.

"Forty-five minutes later, I came to enough, that I carefully put everything back, crawled out of there and sealed up the hole. I can't get anything out of there but small objects, but we have been cutting a large shaft down that is big enough to bring these things out. What they had done was to carry this stuff in there, lay animal skins over it and then wood over that and then fill it full of stone. Why they did that I do not know. I can understand the animal skins, I can understand the wood but why the stones?

"The significance of that it this: In Psalms 77:13 it says, "Thy way oh God is in the sanctuary." See, God doesn't just say things to fill up a book. We might if we were writing a book say a few things just to fill up a page or another paragraph.

"He does not. His way is in the sanctuary. On the day of Atonement, when the goat that represented Christ as the sin barer (all of the sins that had accumulated in the sanctuary for that entire year were figuratively transferred to it's head by the high priest– that animal was killed and it's blood was taken into the most holy place and sprinkled on the Mercy Seat).

"The thought had never entered my mind, but when I saw that I knew there could be no other way, but Christ's Blood had to go on that Mercy Seat. So, type met anti-type and it's

not that many feet from where you are sitting today!"

~Ron Wyatt, Spring 1991

As I said, the day will arrive when the Beast will cause there to be great Archaeological discoveries to be revealed. He will claim these discoveries that will refute all other religions and prove he is the man-god!

Over 500 years earlier, God arranged for the Ark of the Covenant to be buried at the precise spot, caused the Blood of Jesus to drip on the west side of the Mercy Seat, or the seat of the Ark of the Covenant. This fulfilled the Levitical requirement for Jesus to be the "Lamb of God" that takes away the sins of the world.

After Jesus died, the Roman soldier pierced the side of Jesus that caused the Blood of Christ and water to pour out of the side of the Messiah.

> *JOH 19:34, But one of the soldiers with a SPEAR PIERCED HIS SIDE, and forthwith came there out BLOOD AND WATER.*

I believe it is still there today not just because I believe Ron Wyatt, but because it had to be for Jesus to be the sacrifice that takes our sins away!

When the world can see the contents in that cave, shown the cut-outs for the crucifixion announcements, the cross holes, the crack where the Blood of Jesus ran down and dripped on the Ark of the Covenant, it will refute anything and everything the Beast can present!!!

> *LEV 16:14, And he shall take of the blood of the bullock, and sprinkle it*

with his finger upon the mercy seat EASTWARD; and before the mercy seat shall he sprinkle of the BLOOD with his finger SEVEN TIMES.

1JO 5:7, For there are three that bear record in heaven, the Father, the Word, and the Holy Ghost: and these three are one.

Photographs, video, and more of Ron Wyatt's findings can be found on the website for the Wyatt Research Institute at ***http://www.wyattmuseum.com/***.

Artist's Rendering of Ron Wyatt's depiction of the Ark of the Covenant with the Blood on the Mercy Seat.

The Earthquake Cracked the Rocks

MAT 27:51, And, behold, the veil of the temple was rent in twain from the top to the bottom; and the earth did quake, and the rocks rent;

The Blood and water of Jesus, which fulfilled the sacrifice for sins by the commandments given to Moses, poured out of the side of Christ, and ran through the cracked rocks and onto the west side of the Ark of the Covenant.

STARLINK:
THE NEW 5G INTERNET:

There are two big worldwide technologies being put in place which when linked together will cause many to accept the Beast!

Elon Musk just revealed new details about Starlink a new plan to surround earth, with 12,000 high-speed Internet satellites. These satellites are low-Earth orbiting satellites designed to last from eighteen months to five years. When

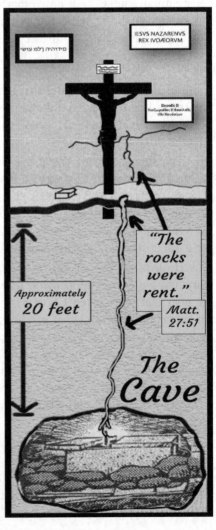

they wear out, they will fall back harmlessly into the atmosphere and burn up.

They believe Starlink will be much improved with over 4G. 4G has dead-spots in buildings and the fastest download available is only 1.4 GB. Starlink will bring 5G and it will be 10 times faster!

Starlink flows through obstructions much better! The plan is to have 5G covering every inch of the planet!

The Elon Musk rocket company Space X just launched 60 Internet providing satellites in 9 minutes! One Falcon 9 rocket only took nine minutes to place 60 satellites. The satellites are round discs about the size of your kitchen table. It fires them into their correct orbit.

The plan is to have 12,000 thousand Internet satellites covering the globe that will link just about every computer chip, especially cell phones, making them 50% faster than direct fiber optic cables! Imagine, blanketing the earth, worldwide, with high speed satellites, low latency, cheap fast Internet that will be 10 times faster than 4G! All easily launched in 9 Minutes from a Falcon 9 rocket that contain 60 table size satellites per launch! They will last from 18 months to 5 years, gradually falling back then burned up in the atmosphere. How wonderful! Happy days are here! Or, are they?

They say only 400 satellites will establish minor Internet coverage and 800 satellites for significant coverage, but their final goal is 12,000 satellites? Wait a minute.

In other words, your cell phone is going to have global coverage. Every place is going to have 5G coverage. That means that when you click on some link there will be no little snake chasing his tail. No more wait. It's all instant! You will have instant access with the new 5G that will go through most walls on the planet. You'll be able to have 5G coverage.

Doesn't that all sound wonderful especially in rural and remote areas! They say even a partially complete Starlink Network could bring broadband Internet speeds rivaling those found in well networked cities. 4,400 low-earth orbit satellites, roughly half capacity, are supposed to be deployed by 2024, and at full capacity by 2027. Their plan is to be on-line by 2024! Hold that thought! There is something more!

"Elon Musk's Starlink 'Train' Looks Amazing, But Astronomers Have Serious Concerns"

Sciencealert.com, 27 MAY 2019

"Last week SpaceX launched 60 Starlink 500-pound telecommunication satellites– the first major launch of its ambitious fleet of up to 12,000 satellites, with the goal to eventually create ultra-fast Internet services around the world."

Wikipedia:

"Starlink is a satellite constellation being constructed by American company SpaceX to provide satellite Internet access. The constellation will consist of thousands of mass-produced small satellites, working in combination with ground transceivers. SpaceX also plans to sell some of the satellites for MILITARY, SCIENTIFIC OR EX-PLORATORY PURPOSES." [One day to become the Mark of the Beast Financial system]

"Starlink constellation, phase 1, first orbital shell: approximately 1,600 satellites at 550 km altitude"

"As of May 2019, SpaceX has deployed 62 satellites. They plan to deploy 60 more per launch, at a rate of ONE LAUNCH EVERY TWO WEEKS BEGINNING IN NOVEMBER 2019. In total, nearly 12,000 satellites will be deployed by the mid-2020s, with a possible later extension to 42,000. The initial 12,000 satellites are planned to orbit in three orbital shells: first placing approximately 1,600 in a 550-kilometer (340 mi)-altitude shell, then approximately 2,800 Ku- and Ka- band spectrum satellites at 1,150 km (710 mi) and approximately 7,500 V-band satellites at 340 km (210 mi). Commercial operation could begin in 2020."

Now we learn that the 12,000 will all be on-line by the mid 2020's but the TOTAL in three layers will be 42,000 satellites! Ask yourself, "What would Hitler have done with this technology?" One worse than Hitler is about to arrive on earth!

NEW GLOBAL FINANCIAL SYSTEM

Now, let's talk about the second technological advancement. This article says there's about to be a new Financial system setup. PLEASE NOTICE THE TEXT IN ALL CAPS! The text in ALL CAPS relates to Bible prophecy and I will explain at the end of the article. Some of my comments are in brackets:

"QFS Ends Corrupt Cabal Central Banking"
FinalWakeupCall.info

"The QFS-system will cover the new global network for the transfer of gold or asset-backed money, initiated by Russia and China to replace the US-centrally-controlled Swift system.

"This new Quantum Financial System– QFS, runs on a quantum computer, based on an orbiting satellite, and is protected by Secret Space Programs to ensure that it cannot be hacked. The quantum technology was provided by benevolent extraterrestrial Galactics. [Demons] The purpose of the new financial system is to put an end to Cabal corruption, usury, and manipulation within the banking world. The key is to implement limitations that will prevent corrupted banksters from gaining significant profits.

"The QFS is completely independent from the existing centralized system, making all other previous transfer systems… unnecessary. … Moreover, after the Revaluation, all sovereign currencies will be gold or asset-backed, ensuring a sustainable value… .

"With the activation of the QFS, the Galactic Alliance will completely destroy the Central Banking System that has been designed to destroy the world economy and put the world population into perpetual debt slavery. The little-known truth is, the QFS has been running parallel to the Central Banking System for many months, if not more than a year, and has countered many hacking attempts to steal funds by the Cabal.

"Little is it known that this new system was invented in preparation for the takeover of the Central Bank Debt System to end the financial slavery and control over the populace. The Alliance gave President Trump the magic wand of taking over the old banking system without changing it. [A new global financial system to bring a new season of prosperity.]

"The Quantum Financial System– QFS, has no comparison to anything that has ever been introduced to the world before. It has no peer; it has no equivalent in advanced technology of any other system before it. It reigns supreme in the technology it applies, to accomplish the one hundred percent financial security and transparency all currency account holders require. With the QFS, the monetary system of the world can easily be changed to encompass gold-backed currencies that completely eliminate the transfer need of the old Cabal central banking system.

"The Alliance had to intervene with OFF-WORLD, or more correctly OTHER DIMENSIONAL TECHNOLOGIES to deliver us earthlings this super technologically advanced monetary system. [Demons] It is rooted in the Quantum Computer intelligence that comes without any third-dimension creation. No 3D creation comes with an all-telling 'recognition system' that mimics the creation of a living entity. It is simply Artificial Intelligence (AI), that comes with something that is able to replace conscious human beings.

"Our planet Earth is a living entity with the life force being the Planetary Symbols. The QFS is considered to be alive with a QUANTUM BENEVOLENT INTELLIGENCE [Lucifer] that interacts with each financial transaction anywhere in the world of finance, to ensure that it is; legal, owner-intended, and transparent. ...each financial transaction that goes through the Quantum Financial System... cannot be compromised.

"Only gold– or asset backed currencies that have a digital gold or asset certificate can be transferred through the QFS. The certificate will reference a serial number on a piece of gold or asset held in reserve to back the currency. Off-world technologies are used to quarantine the gold and or assets used to back currencies. There is no way it can be stolen or taken out of the secure vaults where it is stored. That is why it is called a gold-backed currency, it has to reference back to the piece of gold or asset that is backing it.

"Any fiat currencies that cannot be designated as being clean, clear, non-terroristic, or not clearly originating from legal activities, are disqualified, which are most, if not all fiat paper currencies. Fiat currencies can consequently not become legal in the QFS.

"Fiat currencies already in possession at the time of full-scale implementation of the QFS, received whilst doing legal business, will be exchanged for gold-backed currencies at the bank.

"The procedure here is called 'reconciliation', qualifying the money transfer as being either legal or illegal, and WILL BE CARRIED OUT BY A BENEVOLENT CONSCIOUS ENTITY FROM THE 5TH DIMENSION. [Fifth dimension? Really? We are supposed to believe this is good? Not!]

"The confirmation and revelation of this benevolent component of the QFS, will be the assurance and proof of a one hundred percent benign secure neutral transfer system.

"Without the ability to reconcile old fiat money into the new QFS, all Central Bank activities will cease to have any relevance within this new financial system. Any country that is not GESARA compliant will be left out of the QFS and will eventually be left out of international trade. Non-compliant countries, if any, will be left to barter commodities or work out a credit exchange with other countries, a system that is not presently set up to do business at any level of relevance." [The system which can stop any person from buying or selling, unless they have the Mark giving them access to the system.]

"Each country must be GESARA compliant to participate in the QFS. The Alliance will use a specific quantitative formula to establish the amount of currency available, "in a country," which is to be gold-backed in the QFS. The results of the formula will establish a fair value of each country's assets as compared to another. There is far more gold than needed to accomplish the gold-backing of all world currencies. Once established through the GCR, the price of gold will become irrelevant.

"If the price of gold goes up, the value of all currencies will go up as well, resulting in no net change to the par value of all currencies. The formula includes, in ground assets, the economy of the country, its population– which is one of the country's assets, and a number of other parameters to determine the value of the country's currency. This formula is to be applied to each country so that all currencies will be on par value with all other countries. The application of the formula and the common value of all gold, means that one country's currency has to have the same value as another country's currency. This is called the Global Currency Reset– the reset of all currencies on par with all other world currencies and they each have a gold certificate to validate authenticity. It is the requirement of each country to use the reset formula and apply the worldwide standards, so that the QFS is able to function as planned. That is why a country must be GESARA compliant to participate in the QFS.

"The Alliance has confirmed that their goal of defeating the Deep State has been far more complex, time-consuming and difficult than had been anticipated and planned for. It is becoming increasingly obvious that world-changing information is about to be dropped, probably sooner than expected. This will likely be accompanied by the much-anticipated mass arrests. There are literally over seventy thousand sealed criminal indictments ready to be executed. Once this sequence of events takes place, it will be up to the awakened readers to help everyone understand what is going on, explaining the positive nature of the changes that are occurring and those underway.

"Never forget: the deliberate debasement of our fiat currency by central bankers is theft and is equivalent to counterfeiting. The Founding Fathers of the United States of America saw counterfeiting as a serious crime, deserving the death penalty."

~Sciencealert.com

Let's look at the text in all CAPS a little closer. The article says this new quantum financial system runs on a quantum computer based, on an orbiting satellite system. I hope you noticed "SECRET SPACE PROGRAMS."

To ensure that cannot be hacked. The quantum technology would be provided by BENEVOLENT EXTRATERRESTRIAL GALACTICS. Are there benevolent extraterrestrial Galactics? God's angels don't need metal flying devices to fly through the air. God's angels fly through space and time, at the speed of thought. They appear where they want, and they do amazing things as God directs. They don't have any anti-gravity flying saucers! So, if they're benevolent extraterrestrial Galactics, giving mankind a new computer and financial system, they are NOT FROM GOD! In other words, here's what happened.

The Devil raises up a group of evil International bankers who rule and eventually destroy the earth's financial system. Then the Devil, the most subtle beast of the field would say something like, "I see you have these bad international bankers, the deep state, controlling your financial system. I will help. I'm going to give you a whole new

computer and we're going to link it up to satellites. They can't hack into it and we're going to help you fix your global financial system!"

So, the devil causes the problem, then provides the solution to the white hats. Not understanding that the devil is going to take it over and make it the Mark of the Beast system, we shout, "Yay! How wonderful!"

Stupid! Humans without the prophecies of God are stupid! We can't see the set up!

The Deep State is in a panic, as the people are waking up and they realize they cannot stop it. They are continually trying to prevent or suppress it, but the truth is coming out."

The QFS will be the new GLOBAL NETWORK for the transfer of GOLD or ASSET BACKED CURRENCY. [Notice those words "gold or asset backed currency," that's really important. The money we have in our pockets or in our bank accounts in 2019 is NOT gold or asset backed. So, today's currencies, including the fiat dollar, won't go into QFS! Then what?

Not to worry. There's a plan to replace the evil US centrally controlled system. Yes, it's US controlled but remember the Khazarian Mafia, Deep State or the International Bankers, whatever you want to call them, have controlled our global financial system for over three hundred years.

This QFS is an attempt, hear the word attempt, for the good guys wearing the white hats to come in and kick the bad guys out. That is the plan anyway. It doesn't go as planned.

Remember the great Stock Market crash that followed with the Great Depression of 1929? I remember my mom and dad talked about it. In 1929, there was a stock market crash and there was a great wealth transfer. The wealth transfer went from the good guys who were the Christians, the farmers, the ranchers, into the hands of the bad guys– the International Bankers.

What's about to happen? The prophecies say there is about to be a wealth transfer from the bad guys such as the Khazarian Mafia, and evil International Bankers to the good guys. The bad guys are about to be kicked out and their wealth transferred into the hands of the good guys– they hope.

Proverbs says the wealth of the sinner is laid up for the just.

> *PRO 13:22, A good man leaveth*
> *an inheritance to his children's*
> *children: and the wealth of the*
> *sinner is laid up for the just.*

When does this happen? I am not aware of a time in history when Proverbs 13:22 was fulfilled. So, it is unfulfilled prophecy! In my opinion, it does NOT happen in the Millennium, it happens before the return of Jesus. That means this new system is likely to be the fulfillment of that prophecy! Many people suspect this QFS could be that transfer, but what do I know? Several prophecies say the wealth transfer coming will transfer the wealth from the bad guys back to the good guys, primarily the church.

Prophet Shane Warren: The Storm: Judgment & Revival Friday, Oct. 5, 2012.

(DVD available at **prophecyclub. com** and **WatchProphecyClub.com**)

"I saw the church arise with healing in their wings for this moment. I saw God prospering greatly many acquiring things in A TRANSFER OF WEALTH coming into the hands of believers! Churches became cities of refuge. The body of Christ stood up like a mighty sleeping giant in the earth and began to minister. People were coming to them. Signs wonders and miracles were poured out all over America. I saw America being shaken as the worldly couldn't go to the government for help, *THEY HAD TO GO TO THE CHURCH FOR HELP.* Entire cities became cities of refuge. There was life, safety, peace and the presence of God in the cities. People were running to the cities. Revival arrived. It was a two-sided coin as judgment hit *SO DID GOD'S MIRACLE REVIVALS.* As great inflation caused an economic storm great revival arrived. God will raise up his church."

~*Shane Warren*

THE TREE OF KNOWLEDGE OF GOOD AND EVIL
Prophet Maurice Sklar, May 1995 vision

Over thirty years ago!

"In the first vision, I saw the earth from outer space. As I watched, I began to see what looked light neon lights began to appear in hexagon patterns.

"It started from the North American continent and then spread out to Europe and then around the world. It looked like white laser lights traced in approximately 100 mile-wide hexagon patterns around the entire earth like an electronic or laser spider web. When the lights finally stopped tracing around the earth, it looked like the earth was wrapped in an electronic grid like a geodesic dome, similar to the white globe that is at the Epcot Center in Disney world, only it was not solid. You could see the earth underneath it, with its' blue oceans and clouds and atmosphere.

"The Lord then said to me, "This is what is shortly to take place. There is an ELECTRONIC WEB that will encircle the earth like this. IT WILL UNITE THE WHOLE WORLD UNDER THE ANTICHRIST SYSTEM of the end-time Babylon.

"AT FIRST IT WILL BRING GREAT BLESSINGS AND PROSPERITY. It will seem like everyone is coming together and a new age is dawning for mankind." I looked again, and I saw the earth from space with this electronic web around it once more. But then, I saw the continent of Europe. The hexagons from each nation began to grow dark and became opaque. It looked like black smoke rose up and one after another, each hexagon began to go smoky gray and then black. After a few seconds, I could no longer see Europe at all. Then this began to spread rapidly across into Asia, and Africa. Finally, Australia, China and even America were completely blotted out. I could

only see the oceans. Then the islands of the seas became black.

"Finally, THE ENTIRE EARTH WAS IN DARKNESS– even the blue oceans disappeared. I felt such evil and hopelessness.

"I heard the cries of millions of souls on earth that were trapped in darkness.

"Then the Lord spoke again and said, "Do you see this? Do you know what this is?" I replied, "No, Lord." He said, "This is the fullness of the tree of knowledge of good and evil.

"This is what Adam chose for all of mankind in the Garden of Eden instead of union and life with Me. They could have had eaten from the tree of life instead, and this never would have happened."

~Maurice Sklar

This is the globe linked together in a quantum financial system and goes bad as the Beast takes over, beginning in Europe.

Note: In 1975 the first personal computers were introduced. In August 1991, the World Wide Web became publicly available!

SHAKE EXPOSURE TRANSFER:
Prophet Neville Johnson:
Ministry of Light, Australia
http://www.lwa.org.au/

"A heavenly visitor entered my room a 6:30 am and said write this down.

"The silver is mine, and the gold is mine, saith the LORD of hosts."

"The glory of this latter house shall be greater than of the former, saith the LORD of hosts: and in this place will

I give peace, saith the LORD of hosts. Haggai 2:6-9

"He emphasized the words ALL NATIONS and DESIRE. I knew that every nation in the world was about to be shaken in a very real way. His emphasis on the word "desire" was in relationship to wealth or precious things.

"Then a vision opened up in front of me where I saw this angel holding what looked like a very fragile large ornate cup and saucer. This cup was very thin and fragile. Written on the cup were the words "The Nations' Economies." I then was able to see the inside of the cup and on the inside it was filthy.

"The angel then said "the economies of the world are like this cup clean on the outside but filthy on the inside." I then heard a crack and the cup began to crack and quickly fell apart into pieces.

"The scene then changed, and this angel was holding a large man upside down by his leg. He began shaking this man violently with an up and down

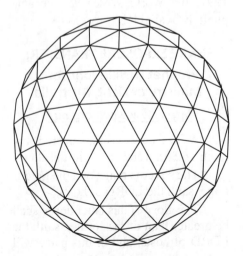

movement. As I watched this all kinds of things began falling out of this man's pockets. Such things as Gold, Silver, and Inventions which seemed to be in connection with energy as well as other inventions. There were cures for certain diseases also falling from this man's pockets, cures for such things a Cancer, Diabetes, Asthma, Alzheimer's disease and many other diseases. The cures for these diseases already exist but have been hidden by pharmaceutical companies. This giant represented the world and the financial systems of this world.

"As I watched this unfold, this angel again shouted the words SHAKE EXPOSURE TRANSFER."

Prophet Neville Johnson
November 19, 2014

"God is going to shake every nation. There is going to be shaking in the financial systems of the nations, and that is very close now, where the financial systems of the world are going to be dramatically shaken. Change is coming...

"Then Joseph said transfer. There is going to be A TRANSFER OF WEALTH to those in the kingdom of God you can righteously handle it.

"...these seven years will see the greatest harvest that the world has ever seen. In the midst of difficult times, trouble and difficult times, the greatest harvest the world has ever seen is going to start to be reaped. So these are exciting times..."

Let's look at the text in all CAPS a little closer. The article says this new quantum financial system runs on a quantum computer based, on orbiting satellite system, and is protected by secret space programs. I hope you noticed "SECRET SPACE PROGRAMS." To ensure that cannot be hacked. The quantum technology would be provided by BENEVOLENT EXTRATERRESTRIAL GALACTICS. Are there benevolent extraterrestrial Galactics?

God's angels don't need metal flying devices to fly through the air. God's angels fly through space and time, at the speed of thought. They appear where they want, and they do amazing things as God directs. They don't have any anti-gravity flying saucers! So, if they're benevolent extraterrestrial Galactics, giving mankind a new computer and financial system, they are NOT FROM GOD! In other words, here's what happened.

The Devil raises up a group of evil International bankers who rule and eventually destroy the earth's financial system. Then the Devil, the most subtle beast of the field would say something like, "I see you have these bad international bankers, the deep state, controlling your financial system. I will help. I'm going to give you a whole new computer and we're going to link it up to satellites. They can't hack into it and we're going to help you fix your global financial system!"

So, the devil causes the problem, then provides the solution to the white hats. Not understanding that the devil is going to take it over and make it the Mark of the Beast system, we shout, "Yay! How wonderful!"

Stupid! Humans without the prophecies of God are stupid! We can't see the set up!

There are no benevolent extraterrestrial Galactics! Demons have been running our finances for 300 years and made a mess of it. Now demons are giving humans a new solution. It will be good at first, then the Beast is going to turn the new financial system into the global Mark of the Beast financial system, "and that no man might buy or sell, save he that had the mark, or the name of the beast, or the number of his name."

We do err not knowing the scriptures!

The alliance had to intervene with OFF-WORLD. Are you looking at that? Off-world or more correctly, "OTHER-DIMENSIONAL TECHNOLOGIES to deliver us earthlings this super technology, technologically-advanced monetary system."

I hope you are snickering. You see, we prophecy students get it! We see the trick!

And the devil says, "Just as I planned. The world fell into my trap!"

SPACE SHOW:

Let's picture this. We are now in the mid-2020's. There are about 12,000 satellites above the Earth covering every square inch of the globe reaching just about every computer chip in everything. We know each satellite has radio antenna broadcasting to earth. What if they also installed some antenna capable of broadcasting a signal at the same frequency as our brain operates on? We have known for years even a simple Police radar can project voice audio through the air sounding as if one was hearing it in their head!

What if they also installed lasers in every one of those satellites? These satellites are linked to a QFS off-world galactic alien computer provided by the devil. What could go wrong???

At any point in time they could cause the face of God to appear in the sky and a voice to be heard in everyone's head! These satellites broadcast down, not just the cell phone will pick it up but also our brains! All the world sees a laser image of God in the sky and hears the voice of God! Hitler would love it!

Try to imagine the Beast declaring, "Tonight I'm going to speak to you and prove I am God. That night, all around the globe in the sky, it's the face of God. All over around the globe, the face of God is speaking to people and it's speaking to them in their own specific regional language telling them the Beast is God!"

This is God speaking and they hear God in their native language. They say, "God spoke to me." He says, "It's true and by the way Allah, he's not really God and here's why …and Buddha, he's not really God. And Hinduism along with all these other god's and all these other religions, just throw them all away because I am God." This is Lucifer pointing everybody to one man. Do you see?

Oh, I know what you are thinking, it's not going to fool me! But wait a minute there's more. It doesn't have to fool you. It just needs to fool everybody around you which in turn

will be talked into killing you! They are convinced you are the problem. You have been holding back the development of mankind for generations! You are the unbelievers! The image of the Beast orders all the believers to kill all the unbelievers!

Expect:

Expect new technology never seen nor thought of to be used in a great global deception! Understand miracles may not be miracles from God, but new technology. No one will think it is technology!

— it to include satellites, lasers, and technology unheard of.

— to see the face of God and hear in your own language; your ancient religion was wrong.

— everyone around you to simultaneously hear "the voice God" in their head and see "The face of God in the sky."

— it to be so convincing that almost 100% of the human race will believe it! Don't be fooled.

— the transmitter which broadcasts the frequency of the human nervous system to make people hear voices!

— the Beast system to implant messages into the minds of people and expect them to do as they are told.

— the Antichrist to use the 5G global satellite system to place lies into humans.

— deceptions! Don't be fooled by pulse microwaves delivering audible signals directly into people undetectable by those around them.

— technology to be pushed to its highest possibility.

— it to be used from space, by satellite, to reach any single person, group of persons, or the entire population of earth!

You are smart! No, the space show didn't fool you like it did most people. The Archaeology discovery, that didn't fool you either. But it will most people. Now let's go on.

THE FINAL SOLUTION: CELL PHONES!

Now, we wouldn't want some criminal accessing our QFS account and stealing our money! Currently, we're using pin codes and stealing is rampant. How can we have 100% security knowing only the correct person has access to all our money in this new system? How can the cabal, the good guys, or the bad guys, make sure when we put our money into this no-one-can-hack-it computer, no one can come in and steal our money?

Let's think this through. How many different PIN numbers do you have? Everybody I know has over 10. I have over 40! We have a driver's license, passport, license to carry, Medicare, we have all these identification cards.

How is it that they can absolutely positively make certain that it's us accessing our money? Answer? Biometrics! What are biometrics? It's things like a thumbprint, palm print, an eye scan, facial recognition, and voice recognition.

I can hear your thoughts now. "I'm not gunna have nuttin' to do with that!"

You're not going to get my eye scan, thumbprint, palm print, facial recognition. You're not gunna ...Right?

They already have it! You think, "They don't either!"

Do you know the new iPhones...? You might say, "Oh, but Stan, I don't use the code to turn on my iPhone. I don't use that facial recognition thing..." You may not use it, but they already have it!

When you use your phone, the camera is on! ...they already have your face! You touch the phone. They already have your fingerprints, your palm prints. They have your voice print! The phone has recorded every conversation, text and left a tracking trail of every location and length of stay!!!! They already know you, all of you!! ...They know who you are already! They track your purchases! Even if you turn your phone off, they still know your location and can activate the microphone!

I had a friend in a high financial position say with a few keystrokes and a few clicks of a mouse he can know everyone living in your house, along with all your family, friends, everyone on your social media. That is all the people you have contact with! Also, all your finances, not just your bank account, employment, criminal record, all in a few moments from his computer! 400 pages worth if he wants it!!!!! 400 pages on just you! They have you! They KNOW you– all about you! Already! So, you will use the cellphone to access the QFS! 100% security! Yeah! Great! Right?

Well, I mean, that's great because now we won't have to carry a driver's license, security or credit cards. We will walk up to buy gasoline, groceries, a movie, any item in any store, and you probably won't even have to take your cell phone out!

Awhile back we got invited to speak in Malaysia. We didn't want the credit card company to turn our cards off when traveling. So, I called the credit card company and told them we were going to Malaysia. The agent on the other end said, "We don't do that anymore. You don't have to tell us when you are traveling anymore!" We already know it's you. No, they already know you're there! The system is already in place brothers and sisters! Our locations are tracked!

The system already has you in it! Some future cell phones we buy will KNOW who is holding it via biometrics with 100% accuracy.

It will scan our prints, face and voice to access the Mark of the Beast financial system! A future cell phone will send your biometrics via your cell phone confirming you have the Mark! Those without the Mark cannot access the global buying/selling financial system!

They already have your Biometrics via your cell phone! And everybody has one, right? Matter of fact, even if you're homeless you have a cell phone. You might not have a house, or a car, but you have a cell phone!

YOUR CELL PHONE IS NOT YOUR FRIEND:

Now, the next problem: this headline is from the *New York Post*:

"Amazon tests Whole Foods payment system that uses hands as ID"

The article states:

"Employees at Amazon's New York offices are serving as guinea pigs for a biometric technology, using it at a handful of vending machines to buy such items as sodas, chips, granola bars.

"The Hi-tech sensors are different from fingerprint scanners found in devices like the iPhone and don't require users to physically to touch their hands to the scanning surface."

You don't have to put your thumb in a circle or hold the phone up to our face! But how many devices like Skype, Facebook and several other programs are already asking you, "don't you want to put in your picture?" "Don't you want to personalize your account?"

And we go, ah yes! And take our picture and don't think a thing about it!

In a few years when they are searching for those not having the Mark of the Beast, we're going to wonder how they found us!

The article continues on:

"Instead they use computer vision and depth geometry to process and identify the shape and size of each hand they scan before charging your credit card to file. The system, code named "Orville" will allow customers with Amazon Prime accounts [The system already has you in it! Some future cell phones we buy will KNOW who is holding it via biometrics with

100% accuracy. It will scan our prints, face and voice to access the Mark of the Beast financial system! A future cell phone will send your biometrics via your cell phone confirming you have the Mark! Those without the Mark cannot access the global buying/selling financial system!] to scan their hands at a store and link them to the credit card to debit card. It's accurate to within one ten thousandth of 1%, one ten thousandth of 1%, but Amazon Engineers are scrambling to improve it to a millionth of 1%."

They already have you in it

...they won't make a mistake! If you don't join the world society, you will not get access to buy or sell! So that, "...no man might buy or sell, save he that had the mark, or the name of the beast, or the number of his name."

The article further indicates:

"With the new hand-based tech, shoppers won't even have to bring their phones. Nevertheless, experts say it's unclear whether customers will be enthusiastic about scanning their hand at Whole Foods. ...China already uses biometric checkout in some stores and noted that Amazon appears to have made a decision not to use facial recognition."

I think they probably made a judgment call that Americans are probably not going to want to pay with their face, but they'll be fine to pay with their fingerprint or their hand, That feels less like a mug shot.

Not yet. I think they probably made a judgment call. Americans are probably not going to want to pay with

their face, but they'll be fine to pay with their fingerprint or their hand.

There it is... there's more. We are only getting started. Now let's talk about the space show.

SPACE SHOW

At some point in the next few years, we will enter into a global financial network provided by our "off-world benevolent financial system" given to us by our friendly neighborhood galactic aliens linked to Starlink, the 12,000 low-earth orbiting satellite system covering every inch of the globe. All people now buy and sell using their cell phones which are biometrically secure that are linked to the new financial system which cannot be hacked. There are no more paper currency exchanges. Everyone on the globe uses their cell phones for all transactions and all the world is at peace! Everyone is happy. No one can steal their money!

Then a man comes on the scene declaring himself to be God! Most people accept him. All those who have not already found a god to worship quickly accept him. He is strikingly handsome and so charming. He is a magnificent orator and is totally reforming the entire world into a wonderful new society of peace!

We know we can trust him because CNN and all the large news networks, the famous movie actors, and people of status in the world all quickly accept him! Everyone is switching from no god to him. Plus, even those who have had a god in the past are switching to him! He is the new man-god!

Some unbelievers are resistant to accept him, then in one night he speaks to the world; all people, nations and in their own regional tongue! He speaks to the world telling all the world that this new world leader is god in a man-body! Everyone accepts him as their God except a few mean-spirited few!

THE RAPTURE DECEPTION:

I love them, but most American Christians have been taught an error. Church leadership lacks understanding in key scriptures and have the events of the last days out of order– an easy thing to do!

In my first book, *"The Secret Door to Understand Bible Prophecy,"* I give more understanding of the Tribulation. Many Christians have been taught that before any trouble, or the seven-year tribulation comes, Jesus is going to return in the sky and pull them off the earth to take them to heaven. After they are gone, then and only then, will the trouble/tribulation begin. For now, let's talk about how a "fake-rapture" will destroy the beliefs of millions of Christians.

Let's suppose a few months after a few space shows were successful, they put up another space show that makes it appear that millions of people are flying off the earth! It is in the middle of the Tribulation, or maybe even later and millions of people are seen going up. They're going up all around the globe! They appear to be ascending and then of course the source of

all truth on earth, CNN comes on and confirms it! CNN says people have just disappeared from the earth; all around the earth! The rapture is true! It really happened! It really took place!

And now the Rapture-believing-Christians, say wait a minute God, you were supposed to take me!

Think with me for a moment. The archaeology deception didn't fool you. But it did most people around you. The space show didn't fool you as most people. But now, the rapture happens! All those Rapture believing Christians begin to say, "I got left behind! God left me behind! I was lied to! I was supposed to go!"

Because now there have been wars, rumors of wars, death and destruction, everyone knows they are in the Tribulation! People are killing themselves rather than living through such tragedy. Maybe now, people are saying, "... maybe we are passed pre-trib. Now maybe we're past mid-trib. Where is the promise of his coming? For since our fathers fell asleep all things remain the same." And now there's finally the rapture– that is the rapture deception. People everywhere tell the Christians, "I see you missed the rapture too. Aw, what happened to you? Did you miss your little rapture? Huh? Did you? Huh?"

Those who were left behind, every single one of them remained. No one really left! What does this do for the faith of the Christians? Maybe not all Christians, but how many Christians would walk away from Jesus? How many become rapture-disappointed? Will they turn against the true Christian believers? Will they then take the Mark and join those hunting the Christians? Some will! How many will lose their salvation and take the Mark over a silly laser show linked to mind programming?– convincing them they missed the rapture?

Remember:

• The satellites space-show to project the image of millions of Christians being pulled into the air.

• News reports of millions of people missing.

• The rapture-deceived Christians thinking they have been "left behind" by Jesus. They will probably get angry because they have been "left behind." Most will think they certainly qualified to go and believe they were lied to. They might say, "The Bible is not true." Their first mistake was believing the false teaching of the rapture. Their second mistake is being deceived again by the false rapture space-show.

• Not only will you see "rapture-disappointed" Christians but expect many to turn from Christ with great anger take the Mark. Don't be surprised to see them turn all their former Christian friends in to be killed!

• Don't join the Beast, take the Mark, or become part of the "army of the deceived" now hunting down, slaying all who do not have the Mark or his number! Expect them to hunt the "non-believers" down everywhere.

CREATE LIFE:

The Prophecy Club radio program started in 1993 in Topeka, Kan-

sas. In about 1994 or 1995, I played some info about aliens on the radio. Shortly thereafter, I got a phone call from a guy. He said, "I heard your radio program. I used to work down in Area 51 in some really top-secret areas. And I thought I would call and just answer your questions, if you have any questions."

I said, "Yeah, Area 51."

He said, "I have been all through it."

I said, "They got aliens there?"

He said, "Yes, some alive, some dead."

"They got anti-gravity flying machines?"

He said, "Yes, some our government made, some from other planets. See you don't know anything. Because there is no such things as leaks with them. The only reason I can talk to you as I have one of their laser weapons. Only it's not like what you buy in the store, it still runs off of two penlight batteries. But I aim it at your eyes, and it will blow your eyes out, permanent blindness! They know I've got it and they don't mess with me. See, you don't know anything. Anything that is on the surface is old technology. Underground laboratories, like Area 51, and others are a minimum of 25 years ahead in research over all of the laboratories on the surface. They have unlimited funding and they recruit the very best minds. So, anything you know is all old technology."

I said, "Okay. So, tell me something old technology to the people under Area 51 but we haven't heard about it yet on the surface?"

He said, "Okay. Successful human head transplants. Old technology. You ever wonder why the evilest people, like George S-ros, continue to live? It's like these people never die off! Why is it that evil people continue to live, right? I don't know if that's an answer but sometimes I wonder."

I said, "Okay ... Let's get to the bottom of the barrel. What's their deepest darkest secret? What's the thing that they do not want the surface knowing about more than anything!"

He said, "Creation. That's what they're working on. Creating life. Well that doesn't have anything to do with Bible prophecy. Does it?"

Yes! It does!

REV 13:15, And HE HAD POWER TO GIVE LIFE UNTO THE IMAGE OF THE BEAST, that the image of the beast should both speak, and cause that as many as would not worship the image of the beast should be killed.

They're working on creating an image that is not made in the image of God, but in the image of Lucifer or what we today call a clone! That is the simple way of putting it. I believe that's the reason the Bible calls him an image. He is not of God; he is not made after the image of God like Adam and Eve. But I believe he will look very much like us.

The Bible says his look is more stout than others. He is a man of fierce countenance.

DAN 7:20, ...even of that horn that had eyes, and a mouth that spake very great things, whose LOOK WAS MORE STOUT THAN HIS FELLOWS.

DAN 8:23, ...a king of FIERCE COUNTENANCE, and understanding dark sentences, shall stand up.

I believe when he said they were working on "Creation" in the underground bases, I believe they are working on creating the "Image of the Beast." Because the Beast ascends out of the bottomless pit. It may be that he is just a spirit and needs a body. That may be another reason they need to create a body. But without question we know that the people who dwell on the earth create a body– probably a body which can be linked to the QFS global computer system containing all knowledge of humans and aliens. He will probably say he has all knowledge and will point everyone to the Beast requiring all people to worship him [the image of the Beast] or be killed.

REV 11:7, And when they shall have finished their testimony, THE BEAST THAT ASCENDETH OUT OF THE BOTTOMLESS PIT shall make war against them, and shall overcome them, and kill them.

REV 17:8, The beast that thou sawest was, and is not; and SHALL ASCEND OUT OF THE BOTTOMLESS PIT, and go into perdition: and they that dwell on the earth shall wonder, whose names were not written in the book of life from the foundation of the world, when they behold the beast that was, and is not, and yet is.

So, we know the beast will look different, but I believe he will look better because he's the answer to flesh, and flesh wants people to look good and smell good etc. I believe the image of the Beast will be some kind of a clone that is linked to this QFS, this quantum financial system, this advanced computer system that is from the benevolent extraterrestrial Galactics that contains all accumulated knowledge probably of not only on earth but also the extraterrestrials. He is able to answer almost all questions. And he says, "...Ha, that guy over there. [The Beast] He's the real god. Everybody gotta worship the Beast! And so that all people, rich and poor, free and bond, must receive a mark on their right hand and forehead..."

> *REV 13:16-18, And he causeth all, both small and great, rich and poor, free and bond, to receive a mark in their right hand, or in their foreheads: And that NO MAN MIGHT BUY OR SELL, save he that had the mark, or the name of the beast, or the number of his name. Here is wisdom. Let him that hath understanding count the number of the beast: for it is the number of a man; and his number is Six hundred threescore and six.*

Okay. So, the space show won't fool you. The Archaeology deception won't fool you. The rapture deception won't fool you. But now, this clone guy is very human-looking. He has every answer and he claims, "I'm telling you the truth. All these other people and their religions– all a pack of lies. They all got it wrong." The Beast is going to give you every opportunity to be deceived. Remember, the thing about deception is when we are deceived, we DON'T think we are deceived. There is only one certain barrier to the truth: the conviction you already have it!

There, it is, the first five of the nine deceptions! This is only part of the plan Lucifer has worked on for 6 thousand years. To deceive mankind saying that guy right there, [the Beast] that's the man god. That's the real Christ. This other guy they call Jesus, oh, he is not the Christ. That's what they are going to say.

DECEPTION BY MIRACLES:

There are two leaders we must be aware of. The political Beast known as the Antichrist which will rule the political world for the last 3 ½ years. We will also see a religious Beast known as the False Prophet which will rule the false religions, especially the Catholic Church. Many people point out the errors of the Catholic Church. I do think the Catholic Church has their share of sins as outlined in the entire chapter of Revelation 17, but I also think there are some Catholics that love Jesus with all their heart. Every Church has problems including mine. The False Prophet will hijack the Catholic Church and use it for evil. Not all Catholics are bad, as a matter of fact, many people including Catholics will surrender their life for Jesus rather than accept the Antichrist and the Mark. Jesus pulls His bride from all nations, kindreds, people, and tongues including Catholics.

> *REV 13:13-14, And he doeth great wonders, so that HE MAKETH FIRE COME DOWN FROM HEAVEN on the earth in the sight of men, And DECEIVETH them that dwell on the earth by the means of those MIRACLES which he had power to do in the sight of the beast...*

REV 16:13, And I saw three unclean spirits like frogs come out of the mouth of the dragon, and out of the mouth of the beast, and out of the mouth of the false prophet. For they are the spirits of DEVILS, WORKING MIRACLES, which go forth unto the kings of the earth and of the whole world, to gather them to the battle of that great day of God Almighty.

Prophet Terry Bennett:

"The governmental troubles will be in preparation for, particularly in Europe, the arising of the spirit of Antichrist. What is coming is called the new world order, but behind that is the spirit of Antichrist and the false prophet spirit a one-world religion.

"I was told it would be a combination of three world religions, Judaism, Christianity, and Islam all brought together into a one-world religion. Those three would be combined as a compromise, a mixture. Each of those three religions believes in one god whereas other religions have many gods.

"The one-world religion will be presented as a solution that will bring peace, when in reality it will be a compromise and a mixture offered by Satan to turn the world away from the absoluteness that there is no other name under heaven whereby men can be saved but the name of Jesus Christ.

"Anybody who refuses to accept the new one-world religion will be labeled as a radical terrorist and a threat to world peace.

"As it goes forward it will move to murder. It will be declared by a religious leader in Europe that this person whom they will receive as their governmental leader is god, when in reality it is the Antichrist"

"When this religious leader declares this man to be god, I saw hundreds of thousands of Catholics rose up and said no.

"They resisted what they knew was an attack against the Lord Jesus himself. As a result many Catholics were murdered. He also saw many Protestants resisting and they were also put to death in great numbers. He saw millions of these resisters put to death, martyred for their refusal to accept the divinity of the Antichrist.

"There will also be resistor nations and tribes of people, even in the European area, who will be unwilling to go down that path, but it was at great cost of life that they will resist, and some of them will resist. Satan is going to push for worldwide acceptance of the Antichrist, but he will never be fully accepted. There will be sheep nations that absolutely resist and there will be people groups who absolutely resist.

"The people of Ireland and Scotland will never bow to the Antichrist."

~Terry Bennett,
www.messengersofshiloh.com

Gabriel told Terry, "You will see 666 [in your lifetime]. You will see the number of man demonically controlled in economics, government, and religion. When it goes to religion that is when the mass martyrdom begins."

Terry told me in a personal phone conversation that the Fall of America would be in the year 2021.

However, both Sundar Selvaraj and Maurice Sklar were told that God had given America a "respite." A respite is a short delay from something unpleasant.

And that if America cleaned house it could have many more good years.

Don't be fooled by miracles. This is the time of miracles. Meaning miracles will be used by both sides, good and evil. Christians will use miracles to draw many people to Christ. The Antichrist and False Prophet will use "lying signs and wonders" to deceive causing many people to accept the Beast, worship his image, or accept the number of his name [2 Thess 2:9-10].

Expect the Beast to perform great miracles and not just healing miracles. Expect him to heal large numbers of people from a distance– to kill people without touching them, perhaps even large numbers of them. Some of this deception could be done spiritually by his devils, some from advanced secret high technology weapons. Don't be fooled. Jesus is allowing this because they have refused the truth of His blood sacrifice, so He is offering them a lie. Since they prefer lies, and refused the truth, He will give over to a lie! They like lies, he is giving them the ultimate liar, bringing the ultimate lies, which will deceive them and destroy them!

MIRACLES, SIGNS AND WONDERS:

Now let's talk about the deception of Miracles:

REV 16:13, And I saw three unclean spirits like frogs come out of the mouth of the dragon, and out of the mouth of the beast, and out of the mouth of the false prophet. For they are the SPIRITS OF DEVILS, WORKING MIRACLES, which go forth unto the kings of the earth and of the whole world, to gather them to the battle of that great day of God Almighty.

REV 13:3, And I saw one of his heads as it were wounded to death; and HIS DEADLY WOUND WAS HEALED: and all the world wondered after the beast. And they worshipped the dragon which gave power unto the beast: and they worshipped the beast, saying, Who is like unto the beast? who is able to make war with him?

REV 13:13, And he doeth great wonders, so that he MAKETH FIRE COME DOWN FROM HEAVEN on the earth in the sight of men,

REV 17:8, The beast that thou sawest was, and is not; and shall ascend out of the bottomless pit, and go into perdition: and THEY THAT DWELL ON THE EARTH SHALL WONDER, [amazed] *whose names were not written in the book of life from the foundation of the world, when they behold the beast that was, and is not, and yet is.*

"To gather them to the Battle of that great day of God Almighty," and what battle would that be? That would be Armageddon. Miracles are going to be a very, very big part of the Tribulation!

What's wonder mean? When we see the beast, he will look so good. He is going to sound so good. He is what flesh, inside of us, has always been looking for. He's got it, man. The Orator appearance. And of course, CNN says, "He is God." So, that means he's god, right? All that dwell upon the earth shall WONDER, whose names are not written in the Book of Life of the lamb slain from the foundation of the earth, when they behold the Beast that was and is and shall be.

REV 17:7, And the angel said unto me, [John the Revelator] Wherefore didst thou MARVEL? I will tell thee the mystery of the woman, and of the beast that carrieth her, which hath the seven heads and ten horns.

In other words, when they see the Beast, they'll Wonder. An angel said to John, "Wherefore didst thou marvel, I will tell you the mystery of the woman of the beasts which carrieth her." Why did John marvel? John saw the woman, drunken with the blood of the saints, with the blood of the martyrs of Jesus. If John marveled, what do you think the average person is going to do? If the woman that rides the Beast can fool John the Revelator, what's he going to do with us average people? The average Christian doesn't know their Bible. The average person doesn't pray much. It takes a bulldozer dragging them into church and feather to run them off. Many will fall!

ALIEN REVELATION:

Do NOT be surprised to see aliens from another planet or other dimensions working with the new society. Do NOT believe their lies. Expect them make open contact. They will probably say, "We are your friends who are here to help earth create a new society."

Before we go further your question should be, "Do aliens exist?" The next answer is a simple one, yes!

In Revelation 5, John sees an angel asking all creation the question, "Who is without sin, who is worthy to open the Seven-Sealed Book

of Judgment and start the judgment of the earth which leads to the seven-year Tribulation?"

Notice the following scripture lists those UNDER the earth. It is saying that humans on the earth are not alone.

Simply put:

REV 5:1, And I saw in the right hand of him that sat on the throne a book written within and on the backside, sealed with seven seals. And I saw a strong angel proclaiming with a loud voice, Who is worthy to open the book, and to loose the seals thereof? And no man in heaven, nor in earth, neither UNDER THE EARTH, was able to open the book, neither to look thereon.

Don't be fooled when aliens from another world land, in some kind of advanced spaceship, claiming they are from another place, bringing great new technology, new solutions, a NEW GOSPEL, and a NEW MAN-GOD pointing to the Beast as the savior of the world! The devil is pulling out all stops. He is going to the bottom of his barrel, using his best deceptions! This is his time to deceive, but we are not going to believe it! We are going to stay with Jesus! The only man who can offer us eternal life for real! Jesus, the only man WITHOUT SIN!

The angels of Jesus don't need machines to heal or fly through time or space! Anything that needs machines to heal or fly, is not of God. These are demons, devils, liars and servants of Satan! We are NOT impressed!

Expect:

—The 6,000 suppressed patents and amazing inventions to finally be released. Don't be surprised to see the "New Society" offer healing of incurable diseases. They will only be using old technology which can be transmitted over a distance, inducing illness, death, or healing people for no apparent reason.

—The "friendly aliens" give mankind lots of advanced technology all to convince us they are here to help us... help deceive us into accepting the Beast!

—Telepathic behavior modifications, which includes the ability to induce hypnotic states up to great distances, to be used.

—Anti-gravity, free energy, cancer cures, and amazing new discoveries to entice you into joining the "new world."

—The "new society" to offer an injection which will correct defects in your body specifically your DNA giving you eternal life!

Don't be fooled when they say they can regrow missing limbs, turn grey hair back to its original color, and replace an old age body with a new eternal body. Don't let high technology fool you. We were warned of this over 2,000 years ago!

REV 13:13-14, And he doeth great wonders, so that he MAKETH FIRE COME DOWN FROM HEAVEN ON THE EARTH in the sight of men, And DECEIVETH THEM THAT DWELL ON THE EARTH BY THE MEANS OF THOSE MIRACLES which he had power to do in the sight of the beast; saying to them that dwell on the earth, that they [Earthlings] *should make an image* [Clone] *to the beast, which had the wound by a sword, and did live* [Came back to life].

REV 9:6, And in those days shall MEN SEEK DEATH, AND SHALL NOT FIND IT; and shall DESIRE TO DIE, AND DEATH SHALL FLEE FROM THEM. [New body or invincible injection?]

Expect a plan to convince the world to surrender their nuclear weapons and all control to the Beast. Don't be surprised to see aliens confirm everything the Beast puts forward! Don't be impressed! Don't fall away!

REV 17:13, These have one mind, and shall give their power and strength unto the beast. For God hath put in their hearts to fulfil his will, and TO AGREE, AND GIVE THEIR KINGDOM UNTO THE BEAST, until the words of God shall be fulfilled.

SUPER-HUMANS:

Expect them to say they can create life and have created it even better! They may say they have improved humans and made them superhuman! They may be able to see in the dark, run without growing tired, have a photographic memory, move things with their minds, and speak without talking with their lips! Expect them to have many of the same powers the comic characters have.

Scripture says they will make a new kind of human. Probably part human and part alien. This is the reason the scripture calls it an "image," because it is not human like the rest of humankind.

> REV 13:14, And deceiveth them that dwell on the earth by the means of those miracles which he had power to do in the sight of the beast; saying to THEM THAT DWELL ON THE EARTH, THAT THEY SHOULD MAKE AN IMAGE TO THE BEAST, which had the wound by a sword, and did live.

Expect them to be invincible, to have the ability to take a bullet or an arrow, then be instantly healed! Don't be impressed. Know this is not Jesus, this is the plan of the devil to deceive!

> JOE 2:7, They shall RUN LIKE MIGHTY MEN; they shall CLIMB THE WALL LIKE MEN OF WAR; and they shall march everyone on his ways, and they shall not break their ranks: Neither shall one thrust another; they shall walk everyone in his path: and WHEN THEY FALL UPON THE SWORD, THEY SHALL NOT BE WOUNDED. [Instant healing?] They shall run to and fro in the city; they shall run upon the wall, they shall climb up upon the houses; they shall enter in at the windows like a thief.

Summary:

Don't be surprised to see high technology, computers, satellites from space, "by all means necessary," to deceive. What if all 12,000 satellites from the 5G Network were programmed to make the entire sky a holographic movie screen? What if the face of god was seen in the heavens and heard in every person's mind and/or heart?

It will appear that God was seen and speaking to each person on the earth in their regional language confirming the same central message. Could people be convinced they had been deceived by their past beliefs? If they all heard from god, at the same moment, with the same message, in their own language, would almost all of them believe? All except the very elect?

Keep in mind, the Beast doesn't have to convince everyone, just enough to overcome those who resist him. The Beast will command all his "true believers" to kill those refusing to join the new order.

Expect the Beast to say, "The Unbelievers are the problem!" They are the cause of wars, divisions, and all bad on earth. They are the reason the earth has not existed in peace. We must kill all the non-believers to have world peace! They will not be ordered to arrest or detain anyone. They will not put those resisting in re-education camps. They will simply be ordered to kill them!

Expect the use of holograms, lasers, and specific frequencies using a central computer to a satellite system to deceive. Be prepared to spot the deception! Stick with Jesus! Jesus is the true Son of God! Don't fall away. Don't take the Mark! This deception will pass, and the eternal Kingdom of Jesus will come in only 3½ years from the time you see the abomination of desolation.

Don't let the 5G satellite-computer-laser-hologram space-show deceive you. The space-show will be one of his most effective tools, BUT not his only one! Be prepared to lose your life rather than spend eternity in torment.

They can kill your body, but they can't kill your soul.

MAT 10:28, And fear not them which kill the body, but are not able to kill the soul: but rather fear him which is able to destroy both soul and body in hell.

Prophet Ken Peters: *"I SAW THE TRIBULATION"*

In 1980, Ken Peters had a long, detailed dream about the coming tribulation period. This is a summarized account of his 2½ hour DVD available on disc at **www.prophecyclub. com** or watch instantly at **Watch-ProphecyClub.com**.

This summary is only half of what was said. You DO want to watch the entire testimony!

"I was born and raised a Roman Catholic. I was not a Christian. I wasn't saved. I hadn't really read much of the Bible whatsoever, except a few passages on Sunday in church. I saw visions before I read the Bible. What I say did not come from my knowledge of the Bible. I'm certain God showed me this information.

"The dream started with a very, very loud noise. It sounded like a car horn from the 70s. It was extremely loud, very ear piercing and it lasted for a long time.

REV 6:1, And I saw when the Lamb opened one of the seals, and I HEARD, AS IT WERE THE NOISE OF THUNDER, one of the four beasts saying, Come and see.

1TH 4:16, For the Lord himself shall descend from heaven with a shout, with the voice of the archangel, and

WITH THE TRUMP OF GOD: and the dead in Christ shall rise first:

"Then I was given the opportunity to see from the heavens looking down on the earth. I was able to see very clearly many cemeteries and graveyards. I was brought very close to many of these graveyards. A very unusual thing to me was that the ground was breaking open, literally, the dirt was breaking open silently and people were coming out of the graves. I saw dead people resurrected from the graves.

1TH 4:16, For the Lord himself shall descend from heaven with a shout, with the voice of the archangel, and with the trump of God: and THE DEAD IN CHRIST SHALL RISE FIRST:

"What was unusual is that one cemetery plot headstones would have a person come out of the dirt and one next to it would not. It seemed to be not just random but categorized. They launched out of the dirt. It was very violent. It was as though a small explosion was in the dirt. It broke open. I literally saw dirt flying, and I saw this all over the globe. It wasn't just in one area. It wasn't just the United States. It was all over.

"The clothes they were wearing seemed to choir robes. They were long like a dress. A cloak almost hanging off them. These people came out in the middle of the day, yet they were glimmering. Their outfits and their bodies were brighter than the sun! I could see the brightness of these people shining out. Men, Although, their robes were similar, the men appeared to be very, very masculine, and the women were very feminine.

"Older people came come out with the appearance they weren't old. You can tell that they had lived a full life, maybe 80 years, 75 years. Their hair that was lost was back again. They looked mature, but they didn't look old. I saw a lot of young people resurrected, and although they looked very young, they weren't very young. There was a maturity about them. As the people that came out, they just disappeared. I don't know if they were taken and hidden somewhere. I don't know if they were taken in the clouds because I never saw them go up. I never saw them go away. They just vanished." [Ken did not see any living people leave the earth].

MASS HYSTERIA

"Mass hysteria began to hit the earth. People had the appearance of absolute despair and hysteria. There was pandemonium everywhere. There was mass chaos, lawlessness and fear. I was able to see many quadrants of the earth and there wasn't any one nation that was under this. All of the globe was experiencing this. It was like every person on earth had just left their mother's funeral. That's how people appeared. They were grieving and despondent. I really wasn't ready for this mass pandemonium, and despair. It began to permeate all of society.

TWO WEEK SHUTDOWN

"Television, telephone, radio and this very unusual communication device was shut down. This communication device was a little white box that looked to be like a television, and was in many, many homes in the United States. When I saw these, they were in nearly every single home in the US. They had words written across them and occasionally it would look as though television was playing through them. All those media devices were shut down for about a two-week period. I know now what I was seeing were personal computers in people's homes.

"The television communications were down for a period of time. Many people have asked me what would cause this shutdown. In the 1991, Santa Barbara California News Press Paper, there was an article that stated: "A single high-altitude nuclear blast by a rogue nation, which could bombard the continental United States with electromagnetic Rays, will cripple civil and military electronics from light bulbs to computers. Military experts warn Congress such an explosion would unleash an Electromagnetic Pulse (EMP) that would erase computer data in banks and the stock market. It would shut down electricity in the lower 48 states– without taking a single life. This pulse would last only a fraction of a second. Our civilian telephone, electricity, communication, and electronic plants are all naked to our nuclear-armed enemies. Even a modest, single explosion EMP attack on the U.S. would likely devastate us as a modern, post-industrial Nation."

"This electronics shutdown lasted for about 2 weeks. Can you imagine all of your communications: your telephone, computers, television and radio being shut down for a two-week period of time? Imagine the hysteria. Can you imagine the inability for a supermarket to contact its suppliers to get more supplies or gasoline? I began to walk the streets in shock at the current events.

"After about two weeks of time, television and radio began to be back up and running, however, it was completely different than what was previously broadcast. The broadcast was being bombarded nearly everywhere and they were depicting a soon-to-come new government and leadership. A man would be emerging to lead us.

THE NEW WORLD LEADER

"The man finally came on the scene and he spoke with great eloquence and charisma. He was soothing and promised answers to all current issues. This man was smooth and extremely convincing. Able to solve nearly all problems. He was a consummate communicator and explained how this removal of people was God's judgment upon them. This rattled me in the dream. I did not understand his position. Let me tell you so you can comprehend where I'm coming from not being a born-again Christian. In the dream, when this man spoke, it began to convince me. It began to pull me into the messages. He reminded me of Adolf Hitler speaking to the masses, but he had a demonic Charisma about him that would literally pull the masses to him. That was nothing compared to what I saw. Nothing. He was able to rally a nation. This individual was able to rally the globe. It was very, very frightening. Almost immediately he began to communicate through large screen televisions that were strategically placed everywhere the general populace met.

"This man's speeches and directions for the whole world, had to do with "New Times" upon us as human beings. New directives for Global Peace and the need to give up current citizenship for "World Citizenship." I must tell you I've been raised a red-blooded American and when I heard this in the dream, I could not fathom it. I've always had a gun. I've always hunted and fished, and I've always put my hand over my heart at ball games when we sang the national anthem. I've always respected men and women in the military. I love this country, and so to have this experience in this dream rattled me to the very core of my being.

"This man continually and constantly spoke of World Order and the benefits of all men dwelling together in peace. Now, even though I was disturbed in the dream, I was also being pulled into this because it sounded very, very good. World Peace sounds good until you see the cost. There is no genuine world peace until the Prince of Peace [Jesus] establishes His Throne on this earth. That's the bottom line. No human being is going to bring peace to this earth. The only human being who's all human, all God, is going to bring peace to this earth, that's Jesus Christ.

"And so, I began to really think of relinquishing my citizenship and this alarmed me greatly. Even though this was a message that pulled strongly upon me, I somehow wasn't convinced of this "New Order." I constantly heard the word New Order, World Order, and New Times, but I never did hear "New

World Order." I don't know why. I don't know if they change the name in the future or if the dream was trying to show me different perspectives. At staggering rates, people were accepting this plan this man was releasing through the airways. No resistance. No one was fighting it. No one was saying anything publicly. I can't tell you if the airways were controlled to the point where you couldn't come on and say certain things. I don't know. I began to go into a serious depression, and I began to ask myself questions. Is this the end of the world?

"The man I saw on the television who could do signs and wonders and fix all of mankind's problems. I will never forget his face, ever. As long as I live, I will never forget his face. His face was almost Supernatural in appearance. He was almost too perfect, and he was, for lack of terms, the most handsome man I've ever seen. I want you to know, I'm a very happily married heterosexual. When I say he was a handsome man, I don't mean that in a strange manner. I just mean to tell you that this man had everything going together for him. Everything! He had this kind of a chiseled look to his face, and everything about his appearance was almost perfect, and when he spoke, there was just a very strange quality about him.

"Many years later, I read a scripture about the Lord Jesus Christ from Isaiah 53:2, the prophet that said that Jesus had no comeliness or features that we would desire to behold Him. In other words, Jesus was not some handsome specimen of a male. He was an average, rugged looking person. Isn't it amazing that the Antichrist would be the antithesis to Jesus that he would have such a persona that it would be just the opposite of Jesus Christ?

"Although he was not actually prideful, he was very, very brash, but he still carried the ability and a charisma about him to levy people into his situations. He was not resisted in the implementation of any of his policies. Not one. No one stood up to challenge him. No one in America started a Revolution. No one. There was no resistance whatsoever. Not on a national level, no one. You know, it's amazing to me in the forty years now since this dream, I'm totally convinced now, that that's exactly what's going to happen because you can look at most of the Churches of the Lord Jesus Christ, and they're totally asleep right now. If you start telling them end time things like this, they label you as a doomsday, fanatical nutcase. Are you one of those guys that are going to tell us that the ends going to come upon us and we're not going to get snatched out of here? [Rapture] Or get out of here without a little bit of a problem? You know, just read your Bible. God didn't take Noah out of the earth, He put an Ark around them. God delivered Lot from Sodom but still destroyed the place.

REV 17:13 These have ONE MIND, and shall GIVE THEIR POWER AND STRENGTH UNTO THE BEAST.

REV 17:17 For God hath put in their hearts to fulfil his will, and to agree, and GIVE THEIR KINGDOM UNTO THE BEAST,

UNTIL THE WORDS OF GOD SHALL BE FULFILLED.

DAN 7:21 I beheld, and the same horn made war with the saints, and prevailed against them;

23 Thus he said, THE FOURTH BEAST SHALL BE THE FOURTH KINGDOM UPON EARTH, which shall be diverse from all kingdoms, and SHALL DEVOUR THE WHOLE EARTH, and shall tread it down, and break it in pieces.

ELDERLY EVANGELIST

"In the dream, I started going for walks hoping for answers. You have to understand the whole world was experiencing this despair, and this chaos that was permeating society. No one was isolated from this. No one was hidden from this. This was engulfing the whole globe. I was able to see into different regions, into the different continents, and everyone was experiencing this. It was as though the world became a third world nation, completely behind the times.

"I met an elderly gentleman. He was the first person in the dream that appeared to be friendly. He looked like he may have some hope, or maybe he might know what was going on. I stopped him and I asked him a few questions. "Do you know what's happening in the world? Do you have any idea what's going on right now?"

"He told me that the end was coming upon us and that he had not prepared for the times of the Lord. At this statement, sadness filled this man's countenance. Instantly, he went from being joyful to being very, very sad. He said to me that he had not been right with the Lord and then he began immediately to tell me God's plan for man's salvation. He carefully reached in his back pocket, very concerned about who was watching him.

"He pulled this little pocketbook Bible out and began to flip through the scriptures. He showed me in the Word of God about my need for Jesus to be my Savior. He told me that I have to ask Jesus to forgive me of my sinfulness, and my sinful nature. He told me if I would do this, that I would be given Eternal Life, and that God's power would lead me during this life. Jesus would give me a victorious life. I said "Well, that sounds pretty good" and I was convinced. I prayed. I accepted Christ into my heart in the dream.

"This man had a small following with him. These were people who had accepted his message. He was telling them about Jesus Christ. A very unusual thing was occurring at this time on the earth: Babies were being abandoned just about everywhere. Almost on every street corner were babies abandoned. Left in their little baby seats. This was strange because they would be from infants to 18 months. I could tell that there weren't any babies anywhere over the age of 2!

"We begin to pick up these children everywhere and take care of them. I joined up with this group of people because they were the only ones that seemed to have any peace at this time anywhere in the whole earth. Some very unusual things were happening with this group of people. It was amazing to me how they could meet people's physical needs. They would always run into people who are in need and they would be able to meet their needs and then somehow lead them to Christ. I didn't know how to do any of this yet. In the dream, my wife also became a Christian. A believer in Jesus Christ, and we were hooked up with this man helping him out. I saw very unusual events happening with this band of followers. Food would multiply, and very unusual things would happen. They would pray for people and people would be healed."

JOH 14:12 Verily, verily, I say unto you, He that believeth on me, the works that I do shall he do also; and greater works than these shall he do; because I go unto my Father.

EARTHQUAKES AND FAMINE

"On my way to make a business transaction, there was an earthquake while I was going to the bank. I was just entering the bank and across the street from my bank was a large tall 7-story triangle looking building. This earthquake hit and began to shake this glass building and it fell over. Killing about 200 people. This earthquake was massive. I know from what I saw that it was a worldwide earthquake.

"If you'd read your Bible, its very, very clear that Jesus said the earthquakes are a sign of judgment. [Mat 24]In the worldwide earthquake there was multiple, millions of lives lost. Millions. I mean literally millions of lives. The world was completely stunned. The devastation of property and loss was beyond comprehension. Some regions were so destroyed they

never even bothered to send rescue teams. That's how devastated they were. This destruction was global. When this earthquake hit, it caused a massive change in the earth's weather patterns. The patterns for winter became summer. Summer became winter, and you might have a day of snow and a day of heat the next day. The world was in total chaos. Predicting weather was totally impossible.

"Very unusual things began to happen immediately after the earthquake. Crops began to perish. There were droughts and famines. I was able to see all over the globe. The most fertile farming areas were totally destroyed with drought and famine. Places that were once fertile were now arid deserts. Weather seemed to have its own mind. This weather was manipulated by the earth being shook from its axis. [Isa 24] How do I know that? I was above it and I saw it shaking. I saw the whole earth rocking around.

NEW LAW ENFORCEMENT

"Right about at the time this earthquake hit, very unusual things began happening with the laws. I began to see local municipalities no longer had police departments. Military police were driving very unusual looking vehicles. Now I know they are called Humvees. The vehicles I saw were black and were on just about every corner and main thoroughfare. The back was removed and men standing in the back of them wearing black uniforms and blue ball caps or blue helmets. I later learned that in 1980, there were no blue helmets or blue ball caps worn by any military on earth. Today we know that the United Nations troops wear blue helmets.

"There was a big radio antenna or some sort of a device in the back of the Humvee. On the other side, in the back there, was a flag. It looked like the guy standing in the back had a big gun. It had what I know now to be a laptop on the dash. They could look at this computer and get all sorts of information.

"They were fairly peaceful. They were not rude. They were not mean to people. They were not obnoxious. I did not see any looters or anybody getting shot or anything like that. They seemed to be peaceful. You could not cross state lines without papers. I saw streetlight stands with little oval shaped cameras on top of them which new the whereabouts of everybody's vehicles.

"The changes took place almost instantly and with complete ease. There was peaceful martial law. Military vehicles were everywhere. They knew everyone's whereabouts. I found out how they knew this. All nations of the world became as one. [Rev 13, Dan7:21] There were no longer any sovereign individual nations. Continents were no longer divided into countries but were divided into regions.

"Television sets not only played received broadcast but also returned signals showing what we were doing in our homes. Televisions were watching people in their homes, monitoring their movements and conversations. The television did not even need to be turned on but just plugged in. Later, I found out that televisions made after 1992 can in fact watch you.

"The global order had no presence of God in it whatsoever. Evil began to pervade every aspect of society. Darkness was everywhere. There was a clear line between who was God's people and who was not. You could walk down the street and you would know instantly who was who. It was not like it is right now when we sometimes wonder who is saved and who is not. This was so evident. There was a clear line of delineation. Spiritual demarcation was clearly seen.

"Television continually explained to us if we would align ourselves with this New Order, we would be saved from all of life's troubles. This is what this man said continually. The New Order had all the answers to our problems and the leadership necessary to bring the change. They were causing the world to finally become, the envisioned globe of peace. This is what we heard over and over."

WORLDWIDE REVIVAL

"I began to help and work very extensively with this older man. This is the one part of the dream that actually gave me hope. Many "so-called Christians" were coming to the old man and his team of people, and they were explaining how they once had a relationship with Jesus but had become cold in their faith and fell away from a life of holy passionate pursuit of God. For a short period of time people were coming to Jesus in total surrender. I was able again to see above the globe. I got to see certain regions of the earth where light rays were just coming out high into the atmosphere. It almost looked like those big searchlights, very, very brilliant. Almost supernatural in appearance. I was given the ability to go down into these regions and actually see firsthand what was happening. It was the most exciting thing I've ever seen.

"I began to see 12 regions in the United States of America and all over the globe where these beams came out and begin to shine into the atmosphere. I saw mass revival hitting the earth. I didn't see any big-name Evangelists or Prophets, or Apostles, nor famous television personalities. Not one. All I saw was normal everyday children of God, ministering in the power like the Bible describes Jesus and his disciples did. This was happening on a wholesale basis. This was happening everywhere. People were praying for sick people and they were healed instantly. They would pray for blind eyes and they would open. They would pray for dead people and they would resurrect. They were praying for the lost to come in.

"I saw the greatest thing I've have ever, ever witnessed. Nothing I'll ever witness could compare to what I saw. This period of time lasted about three to four months, 6 months max. It was incredible. Regions were totally won for Jesus Christ.

"In the Gospel of John 14:12, Jesus said, "The works that I do shall he do also; and greater works than these shall he do." I didn't see greater works;

JOHN 14:12 Verily, verily, I say unto you, He that believeth on me, the works that I do shall he do also; and greater works than these shall he do; because I go unto my Father.

"I saw greater quantity. I didn't see anything greater than raising a dead person, but I did see greater quantity. It was almost as though everybody was like Jesus, walking around, just doing these works and you did not need a pulpit to do this.

"In regions, there was complete light and then right next door would be a city completely dark. There began to be an agitation in the spirit realm that was incredible. At this point, because of these miracles, the World Order began to be very, very angry! Because this was beyond their control to stop. This made the devil very, very mad. He gets very mad when we start functioning in the real power of the Living God. That's when he really starts pulling out all the stops to stop the work of God. This was about to begin to happen. I began to see persecution on unprecedented scales.

PERSECUTION

"Another unusual thing happened. This outpouring of blessing and this outpouring of persecution began to be really stepped up. People were taken to many penitentiaries all over the states of the United States– especially concentrated in California. In the dream, I saw many, many state prisons. In 1983, the Holy Spirit spoke to me and said that He was allowing the Devil to build prisons in the state of California that would eventually become detention centers for Christians. These prisons were being built in rural areas that were normally 15 to 25 miles off of any main highways. I said, "Why would that be the case?" and He said, "So people could be taken in the night hours."

MARK OF THE BEAST

"I met another individual. A very strange thing happened at this point. He was very excited, and he said, "Have you got your identification Mark?"

I said, "I don't know what do you mean? What's an identification Mark?"

He said, "They've just enacted a new identification Mark!"

This started with a voluntary implementation first. You did it voluntarily first. This man told me, "You ought to get yours done real soon to avoid the hassle, because soon everyone, they say, will have to have this to conduct business."

"It was located on the web of the right-hand. It looked like the yellow sun burst of Mexico. You know, it looks like a sun with a face on it? That's what this kind of appeared like. If you could picture in your mind the Sun burst and then all sudden, like a hologram, beams were coming out of it as ray's. Inside of this sun emblem there was another palm and emblem in the web of the hand. This guy was very excited about this. He was very happy because he said, "Hey, we won't have to use these stupid cards anymore.""

"At this point, I began to run to my house as fast as I could. While I was running, I heard in my spirit Revelation 13:16, *"And he causeth all, both small and great, rich and poor, free and bond, to receive a mark in their right hand, or in their foreheads: And that no man might buy or sell, save he that had the mark, or the name of the beast, or the number of his name. Here is wisdom. Let him that hath understanding count the number of the beast: for it is the number of a man; and his number is Six hundred threescore and six. Or threescore and six."*

"So, I'm running as fast as I can back to my house because I'm realizing "Oh my gosh, my wife is there! She's alone. I'm getting to my house and another scripture jumps into my heart. It was from Matthew 24. It was…

MAT 24:15,16, When ye therefore shall see the abomination of desolation, spoken of by Daniel the prophet, stand in the holy place, ... Then let them which be in Judaea FLEE INTO THE MOUNTAINS:

"I began to pull the door open—even though that voice was telling me to run, don't go into your house! I opened it to see the most demonic presence I've ever seen! He was very dark, and there was a shroud of black around him! It was a shroud of darkness over this being. This being was very sinister looking and just his presence gripped my heart with great fear. At this point, I began to scream as loud as I could, and I woke up from the dream.

"I read the Book of Revelation for a while. When I went back to sleep the dream picked up with the demon in front of me again. Exactly where it left off. I think the creature was some sort of a demon presence. It was very intense, and it gripped my heart. I slammed the door and ran off— I realize that my wife, in fact, wasn't in my home and that she was gone.

"I began to run. I got caught by one of these strange-looking police trucks— these military police. They knew my name even though I didn't tell them my name. They took me to this government building."

DETENTION CENTER

"It was a large building and they took me into a room. There was my wife and the older gentleman the Evangelist. They began to politely interrogate us. They began to ask us to be cooperative, come into this agreement with this new government, and everything will be fine. My wife is one of the boldest Christians I've ever met. She's also probably one of the kindest and most gentle believers I've ever met but she will get in the devil's face. She and this older man began to preach to these people that were trying to convince us of this the new alignment— of this government— and so they took us out of there and put us in another room. Now it was a lot of mind control interrogation. I could feel my mind pulled in almost to this order— if we just don't cause any trouble, it will be okay. That's how my mind began to function but yet the older gentleman and my wife began to fight this with all their spiritual strength and challenged them with Scriptures.

"It wasn't like any human could do in an interrogation. My mind began to really be swept with an anxiety and fear because my wife and this older man kept being very bold and "in your face" with them. They took us out, and they took us into this very, very long Corridor. In this Corridor was thousands of people lined up. The corridor seemed to be at least a hundred yards long, probably longer. It was a long, long line of people and every five or six minutes these people would walk forward and take a step.

"Then people would begin to grill people and tell them to renounce their faith. They would never use the name Jesus. They would never use the name Jesus Christ. They would never use the name God, but they would say, "You should renounce your faith in Him while you can still live." "Your faith is empty"– it was Blasphemous challenging these people were bringing against us. Every so often somebody would crack– they would just collapse– and they would drag him away and they would renounce their faith in Christ. It made me very, very uneasy to be in this line because I wasn't quite sure what they were going to do to us. I wasn't sure if they were going to put us in prison or maybe beat us up to scare us. It wasn't made clear yet to us.

"Eventually we made it through three double doors. After the last double doors, we were put into a holding cell kind of a room. The old man was in the front of the line, my wife and then myself. They opened the doors very quickly and took this older gentleman into the room. I don't know what happened to him, at this point of the dream, because they shut the doors very quickly."

EXECUTION

"Six minutes or so later, they opened the doors. This time wide open. The emptiest feeling I've ever experienced came over me. I saw this very, very big man– tall like a professional football player. He had a big satin hood over his head with eye holes to see. My wife was in front of me and they began to tell her she could renounce her faith and live. Now I realized what was happening because this man was standing there with a huge sword!

"It was a very frightening looking sword. I then saw this table that was a little bit longer and wider than a human. My wife said she wasn't going to renounce her faith in Jesus. She began to preach powerfully, and you know I wish even today, I was as bold as her right now, because I'm not. She began to just rebuke the devil. They got angry and strapped her down on this table– face up– she was looking

up to the sky. This man took the sword and chopped her head right in front of me! I saw it!

REV 13:15, And he had power to give life unto the image of the beast, that the image of the beast should both speak, and cause that AS MANY AS WOULD NOT WORSHIP THE IMAGE OF THE BEAST SHOULD BE KILLED.

"I was more concerned about my life than her dying. I was very afraid, and I knew that now I'm going to die. I knew that in my mind I could not do this. I was not going to make it. I was paralyzed, and my mind began to torment me and almost became literally blanked out.

"My stomach began to shout out loud, "Jesus please help me, I'm afraid." But the message couldn't get out my mouth because my mind was paralyzed. It was as though I had the flu, an extreme case of the flu. My teeth were chattering, and I was shaking with chills in this line. I could not process my thoughts whatsoever. It was as though I had totally lost all faculties of my mind, my ability to consciously be aware of what was going. It was terrible and although it only lasted 5 or 6 minutes, it seemed like hours because of the extreme weight of this attack on me. Finally, it's as though something penetrated out of my stomach into my mind, and I was able to spiritually call on Jesus and say, "I'm afraid Jesus, please save me! Help me!" At the very instant that communication spiritually happened, I felt a hand grip my shoulder.

"I was more interested in the hand gripping me than actually what was happening to me. As soon as this hand gripped me, I got very warm and the chills left me. It was as though my mind could now see and comprehend clearly what was going on. I'll never forget the hand. It was a very rugged looking hand. It looked as though it had been through a great deal of work. Like a man who is a blue-collar worker that uses his hands– like a mechanic, builder or a plumber. It was a very rugged hand and it was a very solid hand.

JESUS

"Warmth and Peace began to flow through me. I looked behind me and there was the Lord Jesus Christ standing behind me. He looked me in the eyes, very, very sternly. It wasn't like a reproof or a conviction, but it was more of Him just looking and peering into my life. The most unusual thing occurred to me. At the very instant I looked at him, His eyes were not brown or green or blue or anything like that. They appeared to be red like fire and they were just looking clearly through my whole life. Somehow at that moment, I was able to realize Him looking at me, He was actually looking through my whole life and He knew everything about me. He knew my strengths, and my weakness. He knew every lie deep down inside of me. He knew every deception. It was very frightening. It was a very intense moment. I wish I could say that seeing Jesus at that moment made me very happy.

It didn't. It made me very fearful. I understand now what the fear of the Lord is because of that experience.

"I saw Him in His awesomeness and when He looked through me, He knew everything about me. He knew every nook and cranny. A few moments after realizing this, realizing my own depravity, He spoke to me and He looked sternly into my eyes and said: "Fear not My son, for death will never hold you." Then instantly it was like a kind of courage flooded through me.

REV 20:4, And I saw thrones, and they sat upon them, and judgment was given unto them: and I SAW THE SOULS OF THEM THAT WERE BEHEADED FOR THE WITNESS OF JESUS, and for the word of God, and which had not worshipped the beast, neither his image, neither had received his mark upon their foreheads, or in their hands; and they lived and reigned with Christ a thousand years.

REV 2:10, FEAR NONE OF THOSE THINGS WHICH THOU SHALT SUFFER: behold, the devil shall cast some of you into prison, that ye may be tried; and ye shall have tribulation ten days: BE THOU FAITHFUL UNTO DEATH, AND I WILL GIVE THEE A CROWN OF LIFE.

"Before this individual strapped me down, he said one more time, "You can renounce Him now." I said, "No, He's the Lord of all." I knew that He had saved me in the dream because of the prayer with that older man, but when I looked at Him now, I knew for certain. He is the Lord of lords and the King of every king and I'm telling you, where the scripture says every knee will bow, every tongue will confess his lordship, whether in heaven, on earth or under the earth. When I saw Him, there is not one knee, there is not one tongue that will not confess His Lordship regardless of what side of the coin they are. When He reveals Himself to them, every knee will bow. Trust me, because this presence that He stood in, was so powerful, so awesome, so anointed, so "terrible" so to speak– like the Scripture say, "He's terrible in His presence." Terrible in the sense that you knew that there's no power on earth that could challenge Him. They strapped me down and they said, "You can renounce Him" and I said, "No, I can't renounce Him because He is the Lord of all, and He should be your Lord!"

"When this man cut my head off, the very instant the sword touched my neck, I was gone! I felt no death whatsoever! Suddenly I was up high was looking down upon the scene. My head was cut off and I was bleeding profusely. Even though this hand was holding me, I didn't know who it was, I was actually more interested in seeing me dead there than the fact that I was actually delivered from the death. Then all of a sudden, I looked down and realized, it's another one of these rugged hands, holding my hand, and I looked up and it was the Lord again. The Lord Jesus!

"It doesn't matter what you go through here. It doesn't matter what trial you're experiencing, and I don't know why the Lord doesn't choose to show everybody Himself. I don't know. I have no idea why He showed me this. I was a sinner. I didn't ask for this. I am not worthy of receiving anything where He showed Himself to me. I can tell you that whatever trial you go through, even if it's being brought to a point where you have to lay down your life, it is worth it because of what I saw in my Savior.

"It went from a stern, powerful, all knowing God, to holding my hand giving me the understanding I was His son. I was His brother. I was his Brethren. He was not ashamed to call me His Brethren. I had an understanding, all the sudden, that I was equal with Him. Not as God, the deity, not as Jesus the Son, but as a Son of God. Not the Son of God, the first begotten, the only begotten, but a son. The scriptures clearly say we're created a little lower than the Angels, but there was an equality in the sense that we were brothers now. No longer was it a fearful thing for me to stand in His presence but there was immense acceptance. Immense understanding, like the scripture that says, *"Precious in the sight of the Lord is the death of his Saints."* When His children are coming through death, it's precious to Him. I saw Him take me through death.

"I saw him spare me this feeling of death, even though I died and then He gathered me into His bosom– so to speak- in the death, He showed me that as the scripture says, *"It doesn't appear what we shall be but we know that when He appears, we shall be like*

Him." At that moment, I was like Jesus. An image in faculty and understanding I could no longer see any of my weakness. None of my frailties were known to me any longer. I was completely delivered out of all of that. Truly to be in the presence of the Lord, is to be like Him. It's worth it. It's worth laying down this life and all of its pleasures, and all of its goals, and all of its aspirations just to gain Christ. I know what Paul meant now when he said, *"I will have considered it all loss to gain Christ."* I completely understand that now. I understand the value of being hidden in Christ Jesus.

"The man with the hood, pulled off his hat– his covering, and threw it down and said, "I will not kill another one of these people!" The dream was over."

~Ken Peters

PROPHET DUMITRU DUDUMAN'S TESTIMONY:
Twice on the Electric Chair

In 1987 I was teaching a class on Bible prophecy in a small church in Lawrence, Kansas. I had been teaching that Revelation 18 was talking about America. In February after one of the classes a lady handed me an audio tape saying, "I think you will be interested in this. It was Dumitru Duduman giving his testimony. Half way through the testimony I already knew this was from God, but I was even more convinced when he said America was the Mystery Babylon of Revelation 18.

I wrote asking him to come and speak for the Full Gospel Businessmen's Fellowship in Lawrence, Kan-

sas. He wrote back saying he could come for two weeks! I thought, two weeks!? What am I going to do with this guy for two weeks! By the time he arrived supernaturally he was booked and spoke to one television station, 7 radio stations and 6 Christians groups! I had to take off from work for two weeks to run him all over Kansas and Missouri to speak! Later he said it was the busiest two weeks of his life!

Each time he spoke I recorded it. I typed up his testimony paid to print it and was handing it to everyone that would take one! Much of what you are about to read I typed back in 1987. With all my heart I assure you his testimony is true and out of the 160 guest speakers Prophecy Club hosted over 26 years he is by far the most respected and accepted!!!

"I was born in a Christian family. My father was a pastor of a Pentecostal Church. At the age of 17, I ran away from home. I went to marine school. I stayed there for about four and a half years. I became a marine officer. They gave me about 80 recruits. They shipped me out on the Black Sea. The Communist government told me to search the ships coming in from foreign countries. If I found any Bibles, confiscate them and arrest the Missionaries.

"They said, "Dumitru, if you do this, we will advance you quickly." When I heard I could become a big man, I started searching the ships faithfully.

God Called

"One morning a ship from Holland came. I took eight men with me.

In checking the ship, under a crate of cookies, I found a great quantity of Bibles. I asked the Captain of the ship whose Bibles, they were.

"He said, "I don't know." I told him, "Don't worry. You will know." I saw a man crying and praying to God. It was a missionary from Holland. He worked with Open Doors. I went to him and I asked him for his passport.

"I asked him, "Are these your Bibles?"

"He said, "No."

"I said, "Who do they belong to then?"

"He said, "They belong to your brothers and your sisters."

"When he said this, it was like putting a knife into my heart. Then I heard a voice in my ear saying, "What are you doing Dumitru? I put you here. Don't confiscate those Bibles. Don't you know your dad is a pastor? Don't you know your brother is a Christian?" I looked around to see who was talking to me. And when I saw there was nobody. I started shaking. I didn't know what was wrong with me. I was embarrassed that I was shaking in front of the missionary. I went into another compartment. I stuck my fingers in my ears, so I would not hear the voice anymore. It got even louder.

"Go, give him his passport or I will punish you."

"I went to the missionary, shaking. I told him, "Here is your passport. Your God answered your prayers. He spoke to my ear and told me to give your passport back. I will even send some men to protect you from the police." As I gave him the passport the voice stopped, and I felt a peace in my heart. Then I realized it was the voice of God. Then I said, "Every man has an angel. The angel of God is near you."

"I stayed on the Black Sea for two years. As many Missionaries came through, they came through without fear. I was put there by God, and I would help them."

The Electric Chair

Now let's fast forward thirty years. He was not caught with Bibles. God blinded their eyes, so they couldn't see the Bibles, but he was arrested. God was about to test him before giving him his greatest task and greatest blessing that would win millions of people to Jesus! He was about to tell him America's future, but could America spot the hand of God?

They put him through all kinds of tortures:

"They would tell me to confess where I got the Bibles. Who brought me the Bibles? How I took them to Russia? Who helped me to take them? In my ear was the same voice [Angel] from the ship, "Dumitru, don't tell. Don't confess."

"After five months of torture, they took me into a room. There they had a very unusual chair. They said, "Do you see this chair? We brought it from Germany especially for you! Tell us now or you are going to die on that chair."

"I said, "Even if I die. I have nothing to tell you." They tied my hands behind the chair. They tied my feet around it. Then they put something under my feet. They tied something over my heart. They stuck a big bowl on my head. Then they stuck two things in my ears.

"They said, "Think about those Bibles. You are going to die now." They plugged it in. I felt such a powerful shock through all of my body; it felt like pins and needles were going through it. I couldn't see any more. I thought, "I am going to die." When I thought, "I am going to die," the same light appeared.

"It said, "Dumitru. Don't be afraid, you won't die. Plead the blood of Jesus."

"I started saying, "The Blood of Jesus, the Blood of Jesus." When I woke up, I was laying down. My eyes and mouth were full of blood. They were throwing cold water on me and slapping me around.

Electric Chair Again

"The next day they put me on the electric chair once again. They did the same thing with me. They turned the power up even higher. When I thought I was dead, again, the angel of God came.

"Dumitru, don't be afraid. YOU WON'T DIE, plead "the Blood of Jesus." YOUR ENEMY WILL DIE. You will live. You have to go through one more powerful torture, and then I will take you out of their hands."

"Then I began to plead, "The Blood of Jesus." When I woke up, I woke up the same way, full of blood. They slapped me around again and poured cold water on me. Then they said, "Now, we have everything." Again, I

heard my voice, "the Blood of Jesus, the Blood of Jesus."

They couldn't kill him!

Dumitru told me that the next morning he woke up and all his teeth had fallen out! The electricity had killed all his teeth. This he did for Jesus!

The reason I put this in the book is to prove the warning is from God. Who can sit on an electric chair twice except God is with them!

1980 Judgment Upon America is Spoken

"Three months later the angel came to me again and said, "You have four more years to carry Bibles. The police will follow you step-by-step, but I will be with you. I will blind their eyes. They won't catch you. When they see they can't catch you, they will kick you out of your country."

"He said, "YOU WILL BE EXILED, JULY 22, 1984, AT 10:00 AM. YOU ARE GOING TO AMERICA TO GIVE THEM A MESSAGE FROM GOD." [That was 1980].

"For four years I carried Bibles into Russia. I WOULD PULL UP TO THE BORDER CHECKPOINT WITH SO MANY BIBLES IN MY CAR, THERE WAS NO ROOM FOR ANYONE TO SIT. THE BORDER GUARD WOULD SAY, "DUMITRU, WHAT DO YOU HAVE IN THE CAR?"

"I would say, "Bibles!"

"He would say, "Stop making fun of us! Go on, get out of here." They couldn't see them!

"The day I was kicked out of Romania, all my family was watching the time. JULY 22, 1984, AT EXACTLY 10:00 AM THE AIRLINE STEWARDESS PICKED UP THE PLANE'S MICROPHONE AND SAID, "WELCOME TO FLIGHT NUMBER ...," IT HAPPENED JUST AS THE PLANE WAS DEPARTING FROM THE GATE, EXACTLY AS THE ANGEL OF GOD HAD TOLD ME.

"With the help of God, and the help of the American Embassy in Italy, I came to California. I didn't know anybody, and I was accepted very badly. They took me to an apartment. The apartment was very dirty. Dogs had lived there before. The carpet stunk badly. There was no bed, no table, no chair, nothing. I was in despair. I didn't know what to do.

"My wife and daughter were crying. The children had fallen asleep on the suitcases. I walked around the building saying, "Why, God, did you punish me? Why did you bring me to this country? I can't understand anybody. If I ask anybody anything, I can't understand them."

(DVD is available at **ProphecyClub.com** or watch instantly at **WatchProphecyClub.com**). I suggest you order the **"Wake-Up America Gift Offer"**, as this package is specifically designed to bring you up to date with the warning to America.)

THE MESSAGE:
The Fall of America

"It was late at night, and I couldn't stay inside because of the smell in the house. I was sitting outside on a rock. A light came toward me. The fear of cars came within me. The Romanian police tried to run over me with cars. That's why I jumped up to run. The light surrounded me. Out of the light I heard the same voice. The angel said, "Dumitru, why are you so despaired?"

"I said, "Why did you punish me? What did I do that was so rotten that you brought me to the United States? I have nowhere to lie my head down upon. I can't understand anybody."

"He said, "Dumitru, didn't I tell you that I am here with you also? I brought you here to this country because this country will burn."

"Then why did you bring me here to burn? Why didn't you let me die in my own country?"

"Dumitru, have patience, and I will tell you. Get beside me."

"I got beside the angel. He showed me all of California. He showed me all the cities of California. Then he showed me Las Vegas, Nevada.

"You see what I have shown you. This is Sodom and Gomorrah. In one day, it will burn."

"He said, "Its sin has reached the Holy One."

"He showed me another great city. He said, "Do you know what city this is?"

"I said, "No."

"He said, "This is New York City. This is Sodom and Gomorrah. In one day, it will burn."

"He showed me Florida. He said, "This is Florida. This is Sodom and Gomorrah. In one day, it will burn."

"He said, "I brought you to this country. Dumitru, I want to wake up a lot of people. I love this country. I love the people. I want to save them. America will burn."

"How can I save them? I can't even speak their language. Who knows me here? How will they call me?"

"He said, "Don't worry. I will be ahead of you. I will make great healings among the American people. You will go to television stations, radio stations, and churches. Tell them everything I tell you. Don't hide anything. If you try to hide anything, I will punish you. America will burn."

"How will America burn? It is so powerful." He said, "The Russian spies have discovered where the most powerful nuclear missiles are in America."

"THE FALL OF AMERICA WILL START WITH AN INTERNAL REVOLUTION IN AMERICA, STARTED BY THE COMMUNISTS. SOME OF THE PEOPLE WILL START FIGHTING AGAINST THE GOVERNMENT. The government will be busy with internal problems. Then, from the oceans, Russia, Cuba, Nicaragua, Central America, Mexico, and two other countries which I cannot remember, will attack! The Russians will bombard the nuclear missiles in America. America will burn."

"I said, "What will you do with the church?"

"He said, "The church has left me."

"I said, "How? Don't you have people here?"

"He said, "People in America honor people. The honor that should be given to God, they give to other people. Americans think highly of themselves. They say, 'I serve God,' but they don't. In the church there is DIVORCE, ADULTERY, FORNICATION, SODOMY, ABORTION, AND ALL KINDS OF SIN. Jesus Christ doesn't live in sin. He lives in HOLINESS." I brought you here, so you could cry out loud. Don't be afraid. I am with you. Tell them to stop sinning. God never stops forgiving. Tell them to repent. He will forgive them. Tell them to start preparing themselves, so I can save them in the day of trouble."

"I said, "How will you save the church, if America will burn?"

"He said, "Tell them as I tell you. As he saved the three young men from the oven of fire, and Daniel from the mouth of the lion, that is how I will save them. Tell them to stop sinning and repent.

"I have blessed this country because of the Jews that are here. I have seven million Jews here. They haven't tasted war or persecution. God blessed them more than anyone else. Instead of thanking God, they started sinning and doing wickedly. Their sins have reached the Holy One. God will punish them with fire.

"Israel doesn't recognize the Messiah, because they place their trust on the power of the Jews in America. When God will hit America all the nations will be terrified.

"God will raise up China, Japan, and many other nations, and they will beat the Russians. They will push them back to the gates of Paris. There they will make a peace treaty, but they will make the Russians their leader. All the nations with the Russians as their leader go against Israel. It's not that they want to. God makes them.

"Israel doesn't have the help of the Jews in America anymore. In their terror, when they see what is coming. They call upon the Messiah. The Messiah will come to help Israel. Then the church of God will meet him in the clouds." He himself will fight against all the nations.

"I said, "If you are the angel of God. Everything you tell me has to be written in the Bible. If it is not, then I can't tell the Americans."

"Tell them to read Jeremiah 51:8-15, he names it THE MYSTERY BABYLON, THE GREAT ADULTERESS. Also, REVELATION CHAPTER 18, the whole chapter. There it says clearly what will happen to America."

"Why did he name it 'THE MYSTERY BABYLON?'"

"Tell them because all the nations of the world immigrated into America, and America accepted them. America accepted Buddha, the devil church, the Sodomite church, the Mormon church, and all kinds of wickedness. America was a Christian nation. Instead of stopping them, they went after their gods. Because of this, he named them THE MYSTERY BABYLON.

"So, you know that I truly have been sent by God, tomorrow, at 9:00 AM, someone will come to give you a bed. At 10:30 AM, someone will come to pay your rent. At noon, someone will bring you a car, and give you a bucket of honey."

"BROTHERS, IT HAPPENED AS THE ANGEL HAD SAID. AT 9:00, SOMEONE RANG MY DOORBELL AND SAID, "I BROUGHT YOU A BED. I COULD NOT SLEEP ALL NIGHT LONG. GOD TOLD ME THAT YOU WERE FROM ROMANIA, AND THAT YOU NEED A BED." AT 10:30, SOMEONE ELSE RANG MY DOORBELL AND HANDED ME A CHECK FOR $500 AND SAID, "GOD TOLD ME TO BRING YOU $500!" AT NOON SOMEONE CAME AND GAVE ME A CAR AND A BUCKET OF HONEY!"

You might say, "Why would God do this to America? We trust in God! We have God on our side! On our dollar bill it has "We trust in God." How are our lives? We go after the foreign gods. The American church has adultery, fornication, sodomy, divorces, and abortions. If we repent with all of our hearts, and call Jesus to help us, we will stop sinning. We know that when Jesus comes, we will meet him in the clouds.

The angel also said, "BEFORE THE INTERNAL PROBLEMS BEGIN IN AMERICA YOUR COUNTRY (ROMANIA) WILL HAVE A REVOLUTION. FULFILLED DECEMBER 22, 1989. (DUMITRU TOLD ME ABOUT THE REVOLUTION IN MARCH OF 1988, OVER A YEAR BEFORE IT OCCURRED!).'"

Is this prophecy for America one which will come to pass? Yes, I believe with prayer, fasting and repentance, it might be softened or delayed, but not stopped and here is why:

Dumitru was told, "Tell my people the days are numbered, and THE SENTENCE HAS BEEN PASSED." Meaning this one will not be prayed away."

*(Dumitru Duduman's website is **www.HandOfHelp.com**.)*

PROPHET LESLIE JOHNSON:
Arafat In The Hospital

On April 15, 2002, Prophet Leslie Johnson was given a dream called "Arafat in the Hospital." It was published it in the ***Crusader*** magazine, the website **ProphecyClub.com/** and read on radio. It is also available in the ***"Wake-Up America"*** gift offer at **ProphecyClub.com**.

It gave several events leading to the next war in the Middle East.

They were:

- ARAFAT WOULD GO INTO THE HOSPITAL. *(Fulfilled two years later 11/11/04 at 3:30 AM.)*

- ISRAEL WOULD GIVE THE PALESTINIANS A STATE.

- THE PALESTINIAN STATE WOULD BE A TEMPORARY MEASURE TO ALLOW THE ISRAELIS TIME TO STRENGTHEN THEIR MILITARY.

- OIL WOULD BE DISCOVERED IN ISRAEL.

- OIL WILL MAKE THE JEWS WILLING TO FIGHT FOR THEIR LAND.

- ISRAEL AND AMERICA WILL GO AGAINST MOST OF THE ARAB WORLD.

FUTURE HEADLINES:
Given to Prophet Leslie Johnson, January 22, 2006:

Leslie had the following dream which gave us the newspaper headlines leading to the fall of America:

"I heard the audible voice of God in the night speak the words: ISRAEL REFUSES TO HELP AMERICA. Then I heard the following headlines in my heart. This was the order in which I heard them. Not necessarily the order in which they will happen. We believe these are future newspaper headlines. They are from God."

- ISRAEL REFUSES HELP TO AMERICA

- OMER USHERS IN PALESTINIAN STATE

- CATASTROPHE HITS AMERICA

- ONE OF AMERICA'S GREATEST TIMES OF NEED

- ISRAEL IS ATTACKED, AMERICA SENDS TROOPS

- CHAOS REIGNS AS AMERICANS PROTEST HELP TO ISRAEL

- "IT WILL START WITH AN INTERNAL REVOLUTION..."

• AMERICANS BECAME FU-
RIOUS. THEY WERE MAD
AT THE U.S. GOVERNMENT,
JEWS, AND THE MUSLIMS."

She said, "Then I heard Stan's voice quoting the Angel who spoke to Dumitru Duduman, 'It will start with an Internal Revolution in America started by the communists. Some of the people will start fighting against the government. The government will be busy with internal problems. Then from the oceans, Russia, Cuba, Nicaragua, Central America, Mexico and two other countries will attack and defeat America.' "

Chapter 6
Be An Overcomer

The greatest blessing in the Book of Revelation is to become an "overcomer." The New Testament defines "Overcomer" simply as one who accepts Jesus. However, that is NOT how the Book of Revelation defines it.

1JO 5:4, For whatsoever is born of God OVERCOMETH THE WORLD: and this is the victory that overcometh the world, even our faith. Who is he THAT OVERCOMETH THE WORLD, but he that believeth that Jesus is the Son of God?

Revelation defines an "overcomer" as one who SEES AND HEARS THE BEAST but resists and does not worship him! You do NOT have to die to be an overcomer, but most will. You simply disobey the commands of the Beast and refuse his Mark.

Most people alive today WILL have the opportunity to take the Mark of the Beast! Become an overcomer. Resist the Beast and you will be greatly rewarded. Greatly!

REV 13:7, And it was given unto him to make WAR WITH THE SAINTS, AND TO OVERCOME THEM: and power was given him over all kindreds, and tongues, and nations.

REV 15:2, And I saw as it were a sea of glass mingled with fire: and THEM THAT HAD GOTTEN THE VICTORY OVER THE BEAST, AND OVER HIS IMAGE, AND OVER HIS MARK, AND OVER THE NUMBER OF HIS NAME, stand on the sea of glass, having the harps of God.

BENEFITS OF OVERCOMING [RESISTING] THE BEAST:

REV 2:7, To him that overcometh will I give to eat of the tree of life, which is in the midst of the paradise of God.

...shall not be hurt of the second death.

...will I give to eat of the hidden manna, and will give him a white stone, and in the stone a new name written, which no man knoweth saving he that receiveth it.

REV 2:26, And he that overcometh, and keepeth my works unto the end, to him will I give power over the nations: And he shall rule them with a rod of iron; as the vessels of a potter shall they be broken to shivers: even as I received of my Father. And I will give him the morning star.

...the same shall be clothed in white raiment; and I will not blot out his name out of the book of life, but I will confess his name before my Father, and before his angels.

...will I make a pillar in the temple of my God, and he shall go no more out: and I will write upon him the name of my God, and the name of the city of my God, which is new Jerusalem, which cometh down out of heaven from my God: and I will write upon him my new name.

...will I grant to sit with me in my throne, even as I also overcame, and am set down with my Father in his throne.

...shall inherit all things; and I will be his God, and he shall be my son.

Remember, if any man takes the Mark, he does not get soul-death, but instead eternal torment.

CHRISTIANS' VICTORY!

In my book, *"The Secret Door to Understand Bible Prophecy"*, I explain in full detail the prophecies of Revelation. It is available at **www.prophecyclub.com** or **Amazon.com**. The Prophecy Club version has full-color prophecy charts twice the size of the black and white ones on **Amazon.com**.

At the end, Jesus returns and destroys the Beast, his army, and sets up an eternal kingdom.

REV 17:14, These shall make war with the Lamb, and THE LAMB SHALL OVERCOME THEM: for he is Lord of lords, and King of kings: and they that are with him are called, and chosen, and faithful.

ORDER OF THE LAST SEVEN MONTHS:

[See God's Appointment Chart].

- Prophetic time stopped on the resurrection of Jesus on Firstfruits.

- Prophetic time starts again on the last Firstfruits when Jesus returns on the Mt. of Zion.

- On Firstfruits, Jesus the Lamb, returns to Mt. Zion with the barley, the 144,000 resurrected one-year old sons of Israel.

- This is the "Midnight cry," go ye out to meet him. (He is standing on Mt. Zion.)

- On Pentecost, the wheat who are "ready" are resurrected to the Marriage Supper with the barley.

- The Father promotes Jesus at the Marriage Supper from Lamb to Lion, from Prince to King of kings and Lord of lords.

- Jesus receives many crowns, a vesture dipped in His own sacrificed blood, and a white horse.

- The Barley and Wheat receive a wedding garment and a white horse to return on Trumpets about four months later.

- Trumpets is the Day of the Lord. Jesus, the Judge, uses the Morning-Star lightning-sword to burn the tares.

- Two angels with sharp sickles slash the grapes for the grape harvest.

- After the burning of the tares, the dead in Christ receive their glorified bodies.

- This is the conversion of the living "those that are alive and remain" to glorified bodies.

- Those dead and alive in Christ then receive their rewards including a new glorified body. This happens in the twinkling of an eye on the seventh Trumpet.

- This is the Judgment Seat of Christ. All IN-JESUS report here and receive their just rewards.

- The "Nations" who didn't receive Jesus but didn't take the Mark either are informed they will be allowed to live for up to 1,000 years. They are ruled over with a rod of iron. Iron doesn't bend. If they break one law, they are hit with the Morning Star destroying both body and soul.

- Atonement is the Great White Throne for those NOT-IN-JE-SUS Jesus is the Judge.

- The dead are judged based upon their works written in the books.

- Whosoever is not found written in the Book of Life is cast into the Lake of Fire which is the second death.

- On Tabernacles the New Jerusalem comes down from God out of heaven.

GOOD NEWS

The good news is simple. You can know for certain that when you die, you will be given eternal life! You will never die, nor sorrow, nor hunger, nor have any pain! You can't purchase it or earn it. Eternal life is a free gift. It is not easy, but it is free.

JOH 3:16, For God so loved the world, that he gave his only begotten Son, that whosoever believeth in him should not perish, but have everlasting life.

ROM 3:23, For all have sinned, and come short of the glory of God;

EPH 2:8, For by grace are ye saved through faith; and that not of yourselves: it is the gift of God: Not of works, lest any man should boast.

ROM 10:9, That if thou shalt confess with thy mouth the Lord Jesus, and shalt believe in thine heart that God hath raised him from the dead, thou shalt be saved. For with the heart man believeth unto righteousness; and with the mouth confession is made unto salvation.

ACT 2:38, Then Peter said unto them, Repent, and be baptized every one of you in the name of Jesus Christ for the remission of sins, and ye shall receive the gift of the Holy Ghost.

If you would like to live forever in peace, joy, and happiness pray this prayer out loud to Jesus.

"Dear Heavenly Father,

I admit I am a sinner. I know I have made mistakes. Please forgive me.

I confess with my mouth; and believe in my heart that Jesus IS THE CHRIST, the Son of the Living God who died on the cross, arose three days later.

I receive his sacrificed blood to wash my sins away, write my name in the Book of Life, keep me Holy and save me in the day of trouble.

In Jesus' Name, Amen"

Now you must to tell someone out loud that you have accepted Jesus as your Lord.

MAT 10:32-33, Whosoever therefore shall confess me before men, him will I confess also before my Father which is in heaven. But whosoever shall deny me before men, him will I also deny before my Father which is in heaven.

SUMMARY

The Beast's plan is to use WWIII, an apocalypse so great, as to bankrupt the world and depopulate the world through deadly designer viruses, economic disasters, and nuclear war. Most specifically, the Russian defeat of America as Dumitru Duduman warned. The remaining survivors will gladly accept the promises of a handsome [The Beast] new charismatic leader who will promote his plan of hope for a new eternal world peace.

He will say the only way to achieve eternal world peace is to put an end to the five causes of war. He knows there is only one cause for wars; wars that are caused by the Devil and his men who plan, finance every war thus profiting from them.

The Beast will sell his peace plan by telling the world that border wars will only end by creating a world without borders. Religious wars will only end by creating a one-world-religion.

Economic wars will only end by creating a cashless debt-free society.

Rivalry wars between rulers will only end by making him the one world ruler.

The tools of war, from handguns to nuclear bombs, will only be eliminated when a one world army is created which will guarantee world peace.

This eternal peace plan can only be accomplished through a world government.

The new world religion will be a combination of Judaism, Christianity and the Muslim religion. He will use these three because they all believe in one god as opposed to religions with many gods. Then they will make the Beast the god-man.

Extra Materials

"The Secret Door to Understand Bible Prophecy"
by Stan Johnson

In 2017, I memorized the Book of Revelation. To my surprise, I received 30 revelations, two visions, and an audible voice. God showed him the word "Firstfruits" is a secret door linking the Feasts of Leviticus to the prophecies of Revelation. For the first time, the end time events, can be placed in proper chronological order.

One prophetic word said, "There is a lock that I have put over a word in the Book of Revelation that I am going to open unto you. It will turn so many books written on the end time message into obsolete books." That is this book.

I am called to build an end time army of prophecy teachers working miracles. From time to time we have Sevenfold Miracle Crusades, ***www.Sevenfold-MiracleCrusades.com*** for more information.

Another prophecy said:

"You have a gift of revelation. It's a gifting. It's not normal. The greatest scholars in the world today don't have that gift. You've got a gift that's upon you. I hear God saying as a sign, your sons and daughters [ministry supporters] will carry that same revelation. You will open up their eyes to see as well, their eyes, they will be enlightened. They will witness and they will see it's not secondary information, they will see the same revelation will come forth in their lives as well in this season."

At our Prophetic Conferences, I anoint people with 4 ml. of Revelation oil, which I carefully and prayerfully have blended. I then pray all who take of the oil receive the same Revelation anointing that I received when I memorized the Book of Revelation that will assist to understand and teach Bible prophecy, working in miracles! Most say they receive it.

You can order my book at ***www.prophecy club.com***:

"The Secret Door to Understand Bible Prophecy Offer" :

1 for $20

5 for $40 including one bottle of Revelation oil

10 for $70 including two bottles of Revelation oil

Contact Us

If you want to place an order:

P.O. Box 750234, Topeka, KS 66675
(785) 266-1112
www.prophecyclub.com

To watch instantly:
https://www.WatchProphecyClub.com

Inquiries about our vision to find oil for Israel:
https://www.propheticoil.com

*If you have questions or comments the best
response comes from the ask Stan email:*
https://www.askstan@prophecyclub.com

Social Media
Download our free Prophecy Club App at your App store

**https://www.youtube.com/channel/UCXM-
5jmd0qxd3uLSrvJazfiw/videos**

http://www.prophecyclub.sermon.net/main/main/21230590

http://www.prophecyclub.com/

https://www.facebook.com/ProphecyClub/

https://vimeo.com/prophecyclub/vod_pages

https://www.watchprophecyclub.com/

Watch instantly 300 videos:
https://itunes.apple.com/us/podcast/the-prophecy-club/id679162744?mt=2

Resources

PROPHECIES OF THE FALL OF AMERICA STAN JOHNSON

Perhaps the most important book of prophecy in America. This is a compilation of information regarding the Fall of America. Prophecies of the fall of America includes: Dumitru Duduman's testimony and all of his dreams and visions. Michael Boldea's (Dumitru's Grandson) dreams and visions. Prophetess Leslie Johnson's dreams and visions, including the audible voice of God.

$10

STAN JOHNSON **ARCHAEOLOGY CONFIRMS THE BIBLE**

Actual footage shot in the Spring of 1991 when Stan and Leslie Johnson went on a two-week tour with Ron Wyatt. Don't let the age of this DVD scare you, it is still some of the most recent info we have as there have been no more tours to some of these areas! You will sit glued to your chair as you see some of the most amazing footage of Bible Archaeology secrets. You will See Noah's Ark and its anchor stones; Gomorrah; the rock that Moses struck; giant bones of pre-flood people; Golgotha; and how Ron found the Ark of the Covenant! Great to show in churches and homes. This is the video Leslie and I showed to over 35 Churches which was probably the test to before God called us to start The Prophecy Club. You will love this video.

$30

I SAW THE TRIBULATION KEN PETERS

Ken Peters received a dream over 35 years ago the night he was called to be a Prophet. This is the only time he has ever told of this dream ANYWHERE! He lived through the first three and one-half years of the tribulation until he was beheaded with a scimitar sword in a face-up position. He tells what it was like for Christians. Christians were monitored by their TV's that saw and heard them in their own home! He was shown what the Mark of the Beast looks like. What the Antichrist looks like, and how he spreads his message on large building-size screens. Many events in his dream have already come to pass confirming it's accuracy. Out of the 150 speakers, and 300 DVD's we have made in the last 22 years this DVD continues to be a favorite that people continue to watch again for such amazing details of the future. Get this one!

$30

EFRAIN RODRIQUEZ
CATASTROPHE: METEOR, TSUNAMI & EARTHQUAKE!

This is the biggest judgment to hit the earth since the flood some 4,500 years ago! Prophet Efrain Rodriguez was shown in a vision that a large meteor will hit near Puerto Rico and cause a tsunami 1,000 feet high at Puerto Rico. By the time it hits the east coast of America it will be from 200 to 400 ft high and will go inland with its destruction from 20 to 100 miles. It hits an earthquake fault which runs up the Mississippi River Valley to the

Great Lakes and will also split America wide open from the Great Lakes to the Gulf of Mexico and cause much of the west coast from California to Alaska to fall into the ocean.

$30

METEOR: DESTRUCTION OF AMERICA STAN JOHNSON

Puts together the rest of the picture together quoting:

* SIX people saw: "...a large meteor hit near Puerto Rico."
* FIVE people saw: Tsunami hit Eastern coast of the United States.
* SEVEN people saw: America split into two pieces.
* FOUR people saw: Large chunks of California fall into the ocean!
* NINE people saw: America split because she split Israel.

$30

STAN JOHNSON **DANIEL VERSE BY VERSE 2.0 (3 DISKS)**

Using 441 slides 350 pictures 53 maps and 18 charts Stan helps you to will better understand Daniel the most complicated book of the Bible. He answers questions such as:
• Have the sorrows begun? • How do we get God's protection?
• Who is the Leopard? • What bloodline/empire/region the Antichrist come from?
• How can we recognize the Antichrist? • How does the Antichrist gain control?
• Who are the last six world governments? • What does he do?

$75

STAN JOHNSON **DNA AND THE MARK OF THE BEAST**

What if future science offered an injection correcting deficiencies in people's DNA? ("mingle themselves with the seed of men," Dan 2:43) What if it stopped cell degeneration and aging– giving people eternal life and instant healing? ("fall on a sword and not be wounded". Joe 2:8) What if the catch is people had to get a tattoo and swear allegiance to the World? Would people get it? Is this why REV 9:6 says men will, "seek death, and shall not find it; and shall desire to die, and death shall flee from them?" Has the Bible told us that future science will offer eternal life? Could the desire to live forever cause men to take the Mark? What if something were to go horribly wrong with the process?

$30

STAN JOHNSON **NOAH'S ARK CONFIRMS THE BIBLE**

Recorded Oct 2012: In 1991 Stan and Leslie went on a two week tour with Ron Wyatt to see archaeological evidence to prove: Noah's Ark; the crossing site of the Red Sea; Jesus' tomb and many other amazing discoveries. If the existence of Noah's Ark were a proven fact, it would confirm the accuracy of the Bible. The devil knows it has

been found so his only defense is to present decoys; so many in fact, that unless a person has taken the time to investigate the evidence they would write off the genuine from frustration and confusion. For those who would like some real solid evidence to confirm the accuracy of the Bible, you will love this video.

$20

REVELATIONS FOR THE **MIDNIGHT HOUR** MAURICE SKLAR

At age four, Maurice was a child prodigy playing the violin. He won numerous awards and studied with the best. Maurice has appeared as a soloist with many orchestras and concerts across the country and abroad. Maurice teaches the Word of God and flows in healing and the prophetic. He is a modern-day psalmist with his violin. In 1985 God began to speak to him in dreams and visions. He will share ten visions of America's fall and the endtimes.

TOPICS:

* America the Victorian Mansion * Tree of Knowledge of Good and Evil

* Gates of Grace Closing * The Six Babylons

* Prophecy - December 1, 2011 * The Wedding Supper

$30

SHANE WARREN **THE STORM: JUDGMENT AND REVIVAL**

Shane was miraculously called to preach at the age of twelve by a supernatural visitation. He is respected inter-denominationally for his teaching / preaching and church growth philosophies.

He was shown visions of America:

* Iran, Russia and China Conspire to Kill Dollar. * The Dollar Will be Worthless.

* New Madrid Earthquake Divides America * "They Divided My Land, Now I Will Divide Their Land."

* Silver Will Rise Far More than Gold. * Major Riots Across the U.S.A.

* People Will Demand Entitlements * Many Will Return to the Church

$30

DOUG METZGER **WILL YOU SURVIVE AMERICA'S FALL?**

At the age of 19 Doug had a very radical salvation and immediately saw visions. He was show 12 cities that would be hit by suitcase nuclear devices and he saw what happened afterward. This is probably the second snake bite shown to M. Boldea. He was show what will happen when America falls and how many will give up and die. He was shown how many who are saved now will fall away due to no depth of root in the LORD. Very good! Doug was shown unspeakable torment is coming to turn America back to God.

* America the Fallen Tree * 10 to 1 Dollar Devaluation * Dollar Becomes Worthless

* Vision of Nuclear Missile * Visions of the End of America * The Great Betrayal

$30

**Get everything on pages 82–84
valued at $345, for a gift of $150
at ProphecyClub.com**